Hal Leonard

GUITAR METHOD

BEGINNING GUITAR

SUPERBOOK

BY WILL SCHMID

HAL•LEONARD®
CORPORATION

7777 W. BLUEMOUND RD. P.O. BOX 13819 MILWAUKEE, WI 53213

BEGINNING GUITAR
SUPERBOOK

CONTENTS

How To Use The Superbook 4

Hal Leonard Guitar Method - Book 1

Foreword 6
Your Guitar 6
Tuning 7
Playing Position 8
Musical Symbols 9
Notes on the First String 10
Notes on the Second String 12
    ODE TO JOY 14
    ROUND 14
Notes on the Third String 15
    YANKEE DOODLE 16
    THE BELLS (Duet) 16
    AU CLAIR DE LA LUNE (Duet) 17
    AURA LEE 18
    HE'S A JOLLY GOOD FELLOW 18
3-String Chords - C, G, G7 19
Guitar Solos 20
    MARIANNE 20
    DOWN IN THE VALLEY 20
Notes on the Fourth String 21
    THE RIDDLE SONG 22
The D7 Chord 23
    12-BAR BLUES-ROCK 23
    WORRIED MAN BLUES 24
    AMAZING GRACE 24
    WHEN THE SAINTS GO MARCHING IN 25
    THE GYPSY GUITAR 25
Notes on the Fifth String 26
    BLUE BASS 26
    THE VOLGA BOATMAN 27
    GREENSLEEVES 27
Notes on the Sixth String 28
    JOHNNY HAS GONE FOR A SOLDIER 29
    BASS ROCK 29

Half and Whole Steps 30
F-sharp 30
    LONDONDERRY AIR 30
Key Signatures 31
    SHENANDOAH (Duet) 31
Rests 32
    ROCK 'N' REST 33
    JACK STUART 33
The Full C, G and G7 Chords 34
    WILL THE CIRCLE BE UNBROKEN 36
    CORINNA 36
    IRISH TUNE 37
The Bass Note/Strum 37
Eighth Notes 38
    DRUNKEN SAILOR 39
    FRERE JACQUES 39
    SAILORS HORNPIPE 39
    BOOGIE BASS 40
    3-PART ROUND 40
The E Minor Chord 41
    HEY, HO, NOBODY HOME 41
    SHALOM CHAVERIM 41
    MOLLY MALONE 42
More Advanced Strums 43
    SIMPLE GIFTS 44
Bass-Melody Solos 46
    ROW, ROW, ROW YOUR BOAT 46
    WORRIED MAN BLUES 46
    WHEN THE SAINTS GO MARCHING IN 47
New Note - C# 47
    MINUET IN G (Duet) 48
    GUITAR ENSEMBLE 50
Chord Chart 51

Easy Pop Melodies

MULL OF KINTYRE 54
WHEN I NEED YOU 55
LET IT BE 56
HOUSE OF THE RISING SUN 57
BOOK OF LOVE 58
DON'T BE CRUEL 59
ALL MY LOVING 60
SCARBOROUGH FAIR 61
LOVE ME TENDER 62
BYE BYE LOVE 63

NOWHERE MAN 64
NORWEGIAN WOOD 65
EVERY BREATH YOU TAKE 66
YELLOW SUBMARINE 67
YOUR SONG 68
AT THE HOP 70
LOW RIDER 71
MAGGIE MAY 72
IMAGINE 74
THE MASTERPIECE 76

The Chord Strummer

Foreword 78
How to Use This Book 79
Playing Chords 80
The C and G7 Chords 80
   ROCK-A-MY SOUL 81
   HE'S GOT THE WHOLE WORLD IN HIS HANDS 81
The G and D7 Chords 82
   TOM DOOLEY 83
   DOWN IN THE VALLEY 83
   THIS LITTLE LIGHT OF MINE 84
   THIS LAND IS YOUR LAND 85
Strum Variations 86
   HOUND DOG 87
The Capo 88
The Em Chord 88
   ELEANOR RIGBY 89
   TELL OL' BILL 90
   WHERE HAVE ALL THE FLOWERS GONE? 91
The Syncopated Strum 92
   THE MIDNIGHT SPECIAL 93
2-Beat Strums 94
   IF I HAD A HAMMER 95
The D and A7 Chords 96
   TULSA TIME 97
   A PLACE IN THE CHOIR 98

The Bass Note/After Strum 99
   GOODNIGHT IRENE 100
The Em7 Chord 101
   CIRCLES 101
The Am Chord 102
   SIXTEEN TONS 102
The Am7 Chord 104
   FIRE AND RAIN 104
The Dm Chord 106
   THE DRUNKEN SAILOR 106
Finger Picking 107
   THE WORRIED MAN BLUES 108
   SCARBOROUGH FAIR 109
The A Chord 110
   YELLOW SUBMARINE 110
The E Chord 112
   HEY JUDE 112
   THE RAINBOW CONNECTION 114
The B7 Chord 116
   RAMBLIN' ROUND 116
The E7 Chord 117
   GOOD MORNIN' BLUES 117
The F Chord 118
   YOU NEEDED ME 118

Easy Chord Trax

ROCK AROUND THE CLOCK 122
LOVE ME DO 124
PEGGY SUE 126
BIRD DOG 128
CANDLE IN THE WIND 130
LONG TALL SALLY 132
ELEANOR RIGBY 133

TAKIN' CARE OF BUSINESS 134
SURFIN' U.S.A. 136
BLUE SUEDE SHOES 138
AFRICA UNITE 140
DUKE OF EARL 142
Chord/Strum Chart 143

Rock Trax - 1

How to Use Rock Trax – Book and CD 146
Rock Trax #1 147
  Rhythm Guitar: E, Em, E Power Chord 147
  Lead Guitar: E G B D 148
  Solo Licks: Building Improvisations 149
Rock Trax #2 150
  Rhythm Guitar: A, Am A7, A Power Chord 150
  Lead Guitar: E Minor Pentatonic (Blues/Rock) ...151
  The Slide 152
  Solo Licks: Improvising on the Em Pentatonic ...153
  Bending Notes 154
Major Scales and Major Chords 155
  Half Step, Whole Step; Root, Third, Fifth
Minor Scales and Minor Chords 156
  Flats, Sharps, Naturals
Rock Trax #3 157
  Rhythm Guitar: E7, A7 and B7 Bar chords,
          B Power Chord 157
  Lead Guitar and Solo Licks: 12-Bar Blues/Rock in E 158
Rock Trax #4 159
  Rhythm Guitar: A and D7 Bar Chords,
          E7, D Power Chord 159
  Lead Guitar: A Minor Pentatonic 160
  Solo Licks: 12-Bar Blues/Rock in A 161
The Complete Fretboard 162

Rock Trax #5 163
  Rhythm Guitar: Am and G Bar Chords, G,
          G Power Chord 163
  Lead Guitar: The Major Pentatonic 164
  The Hammer-on and Pull-off (slur) 165
  Solo Licks: Improvising from Chords – Am and G ...166
Rock Trax #6 167
  Rhythm Guitar: G(add9), Em(add9) 167
  Lead Guitar: Relative Minors and Majors: Em, G ...168
  Solo Licks: Improvising from Chords – Em and G ...169
Rock Trax #7 170
  Rhythm Guitar: D, C, D(add9), C(add9) 170
  Lead Guitar: C and D Major 171
  Solo Licks: Improvising from C and D 172
Rock Trax #8 173
  Rhythm Guitar: A, G, D 173
  Lead Guitar: A Major 173
  Solo Licks: Improvising from A, G and D 174

HOW TO USE THE SUPERBOOK

The *Hal Leonard Guitar Method* began with just three books, but over the years it has evolved into a complete system of related methods and supplements. Now, for the first time, you have all of the beginning books and CDs in one super package. This combination of resources allows you to start learning to play guitar in a way that builds total musicianship — a well-rounded balance of skills and knowledge. This book is based on years of teaching guitar students of all ages, and it also reflects some of the best guitar teaching ideas from around the world. Because all guitar players learn differently, you can chart your own path through this book to suit your needs. Although many of the lessons in this book are self-explanatory, a good guitar teacher helps.

This product is available as a **BOOK ONLY**, and as a **BOOK/CD PACKAGE** (CD's for four of the five sections). If you are working on a piece with both melody and chords, you may play one part at a time; sing and play at the same time; tape record one part and play along with it; or play with other guitarists.

You may begin either **playing notes** or **playing chords**, but a mixture of these is probably best.

Playing Notes: Learning to read and play instrumental guitar

- Use the *Hal Leonard Guitar Method Book 1* (p. 5) as your starting point; then when you have progressed through notes on the 3rd string, supplement it with *Easy Pop Melodies* (p. 53). This will give you a good mixture of traditional and pop/rock tunes to play.
- Single-note melodies can be played with a pick or with the thumb or fingers.
- Play each exercise and song carefully and steadily. Repeat each piece until you can play it with ease before going on.
- Keep a steady beat by tapping your foot (toe) or by playing along with a metronome.

Playing Chords: Strumming chords as you sing or whistle the melody

- Use *The Chord Strummer* (p.77) as your introduction to playing chords. As you progress, you may supplement this new skill by singing and strumming chords to the rock songs in *Easy Chord Trax*.
- Study each new chord diagram carefully. If there are optional ways to play a chord, begin with the easiest and then work on the harder form when you are ready. Carefully follow the suggested fingerings in the book.
- Try to sing (or whistle) the melodies and play the chords along with your singing. This is a good way to find out how automatic your chord ability is. Most good guitar players sing and play; develop this dimension of your talent.
- The first responsibility of a chord player is to **play the right chord on time**. Keep this in mind as you learn new strumming or finger picking patterns. No matter how concerned you might be with right-hand patterns, getting to the correct chord with your left hand is more important. If necessary, leave the old chord early in order to arrive at the new chord on time.

Learning new songs and pieces

- When learning a new song or instrumental piece, first look through the piece to see if you remember the chords or the notes used in that piece. Begin at a slower speed, use simple strums until the chords are learned; then proceed to more difficult techniques.
- On pages where you are learning the melody, first play through the notes; then try singing the lyrics.

Improvising and writing your own music

- Use *Rock Trax-1* (p. 145) to get started with creating your own music. *Rock Trax-1* begins at an easy level with no-fault improvisation — you can't play a wrong note. It then progresses into 12-bar blues which will lead you right into rock leads and power chords. Practice playing the "Rock Strum" for each Trax and record it if you have a tape recorder; then practice the lead guitar "Solo Licks" and scales that will help you put together your own solos. You may play solos along with the taped "Rock Strum" or with another player. If two guitars play together, alternating rhythm and lead guitar roles is a fun challenge.
- As you learn how melodies and chords combine, try making up your own songs or instrumental solos. You can either tape record them, write them down on paper, or sequence them on a MIDI compatible computer.

Playing with others

- Throughout the five parts of the *Beginning Guitar Superbook* you will find many opportunities to join with other guitarists, bass players, singers and musicians to make ensemble music — to form your own group.
- Playing and singing with others reinforces the need to play without stopping, to listen for balance and to be sensitive to what others are doing. It is a great way to feed your interest in guitar.

Will Schmid

BOOK 1

Hal Leonard
GUITAR METHOD™

FOREWORD

Since the first edition of this method was published in 1977, I have talked with thousands of guitar teachers about how the method worked for them. This feedback has been essential in building supplements to the method and a catalog with real integrity. When I decided to revise Book 1, I sent out a survey to a panel of leading guitar teachers, who answered a series of questions and marked up the book. In your hands is the fruit of our labors, and a further reason why the Hal Leonard Guitar Method (published in 8 languages) will gain wider acceptance by teachers and students. Thanks to Kirk Likes, Larry Beekman, Jim Skinger, Harold Hooper, Jim Cooney, John Campbell, George Widiger, Mike Alwin, John Dragonetti, Tony Collova, Gary Wolk and Debi Kossoris.

Will Schmid

YOUR GUITAR

This book is designed for use with any type of guitar — acoustic steel-string, nylon-string classic or electric. Any of these guitars can be adapted to use in a wide variety of styles of music.

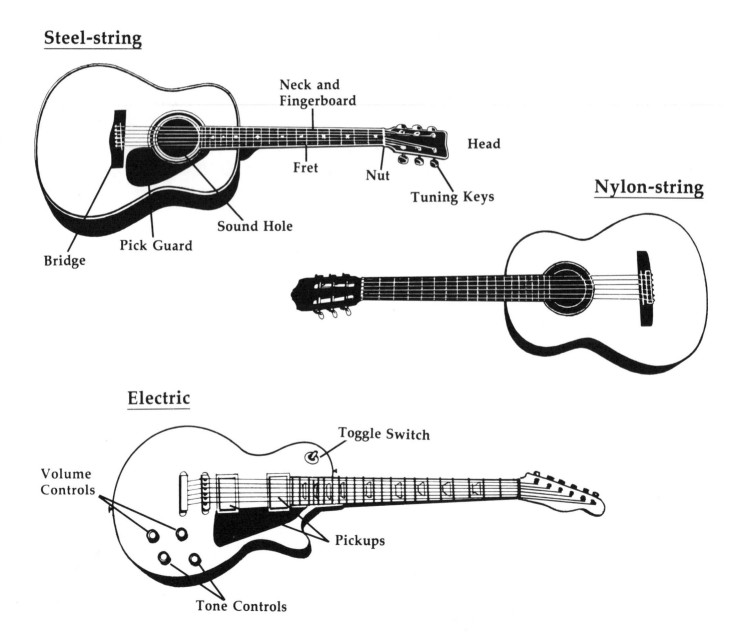

Steel-string

Neck and Fingerboard
Head
Fret
Nut
Tuning Keys
Sound Hole
Pick Guard
Bridge

Nylon-string

Electric

Toggle Switch
Volume Controls
Pickups
Tone Controls

TUNING (Indicates Audio Track Number)

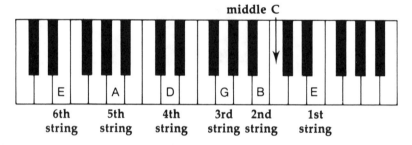

TUNING KEYS

1—E
2—B
3—G
4—D
5—A
6—E

Tuning to a Piano

When you are tuning your guitar, you will adjust the pitch (highness or lowness of sound) of each string by turning the corresponding tuning key. Tightening a string raises the pitch and loosening it lowers the pitch.

The strings are numbered 1 through 6 beginning with the thinnest string, the one closest to your knee. Tune each string in sequence beginning with the **sixth** string, by playing the correct key on the piano (see diagram) and slowly turning the tuning key until the sound of the string matches the sound of the piano.

Tuning with an Electronic Guitar Tuner

An electronic tuner "reads" the pitch of a sound and tells you whether or not the pitch is correct. Until your ear is well trained in hearing pitches, this can be a much more accurate way to tune. There are many different types of tuners available, and each one will come with more detailed instructions for its use.

Keyboard

middle C

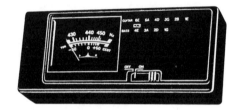

E	A	D	G	B	E
6th string	5th string	4th string	3rd string	2nd string	1st string

Relative Tuning

To check or correct your tuning when no pitch source is available, follow these steps:

• Assume that the sixth string is tuned correctly to E.

• Press the sixth string at the 5th fret. This is the pitch A to which you tune your open fifth string. Play the depressed sixth string and the fifth string with your thumb. When the two sounds match, you are in tune.

• Press the fifth string at the 5th fret and tune the open fourth string to it. Follow the same procedure that you did on the fifth and sixth strings.

• Press the fourth string at the 5th fret and tune the open third string to it.

• To tune the second string, press the third string at the 4th fret and tune the open second string to it.

• Press the second string at the 5th fret and tune the first string to it.

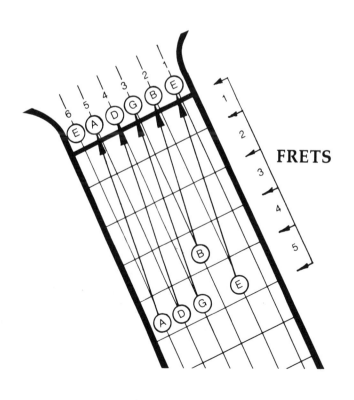

FRETS

PLAYING POSITION

There are several ways to hold the guitar comfortably. On the left is a typical seated position, and on the right is the standing position. Observe the following general guidelines in forming your playing posture:

- Position your body, arms and legs in such a way that you **avoid tension.**

- If you feel tension creeping into your playing, you probably need to reassess your position.

- Tilt the neck upwards—never down.

- Keep the body of the guitar as vertical as possible. Avoid slanting the top of the guitar so that you can see better. Balance your weight evenly from left to right. Sit straight (but not rigid).

Left-hand fingers are numbered 1 through 4. (Pianists: Note that the thumb is not number 1.) Place the thumb in back of the neck roughly opposite the 2nd finger as shown below. Avoid gripping the neck like a baseball bat with the palm touching the back of the neck.

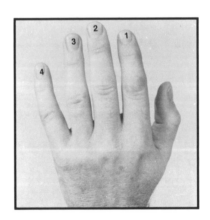

These photos show the position for holding a pick and the right-hand position in relationship to the strings. Strive for finger efficiency and relaxation in your playing.

MUSICAL SYMBOLS

Music is written in **notes** on a **staff.** The staff has five lines and four spaces between the lines. Where a note is written on the staff determines its **pitch** (highness or lowness). At the beginning of the staff is a **clef sign.** Guitar music is written in the treble clef.

Each line and space of the staff has a letter name: The **lines** are, (from bottom to top) E - G - B - D - F (which you can remember as Every Guitarist Begins Doing Fine): The spaces are from bottom to top, F - A - C - E, which spells "Face."

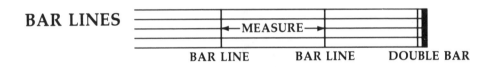

The staff is divided into several parts by bar lines. The space between two bar lines is called a measure. To end a piece of music a double bar is placed on the staff.

Each measure contains a group of beats. Beats are the steady pulse of music. You respond to the pulse or beat when you tap your foot.

Notes indicate the length (number of counts) of musical sound.

When different kinds of notes are placed on different lines or spaces, you will know the pitch of the note and how long to play the sound.

NOTES ON THE FIRST STRING

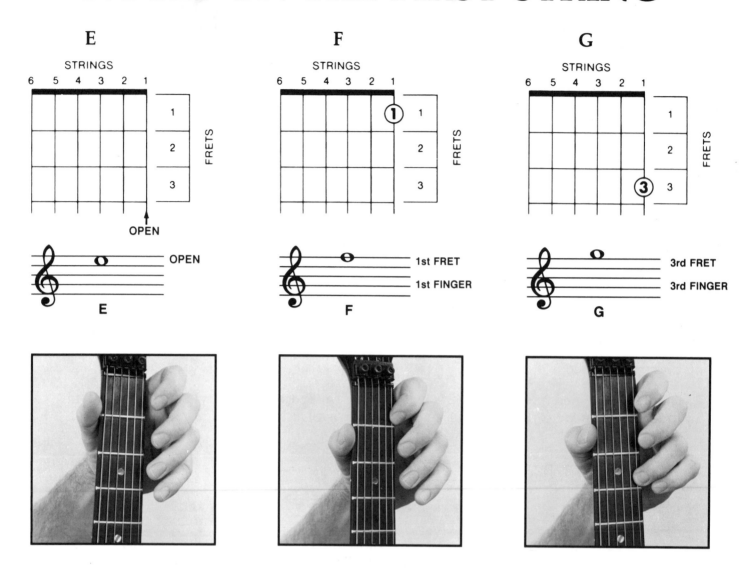

This sign (⊓) tells you to strike the string with a downward motion of the pick.

At first practice the exercises slowly and steadily. When you can play them well at a slow speed, gradually increase the tempo (speed).

Touch only the tips of the fingers on the strings.

Keep the left hand fingers arched over the strings.

Some songs are longer than one line. When you reach the end of the first line of music, continue on to the second line without stopping. Grey letters above the staff indicate chords to be played by your teacher. Measure numbers are given at the beginning of each new line of music.

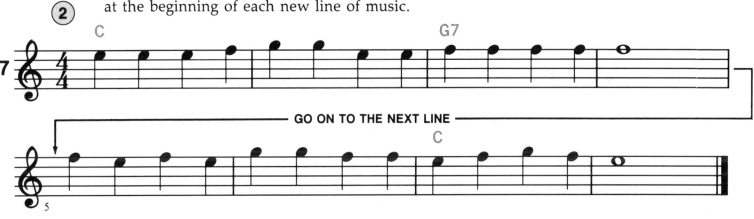

11

NOTES ON THE SECOND STRING

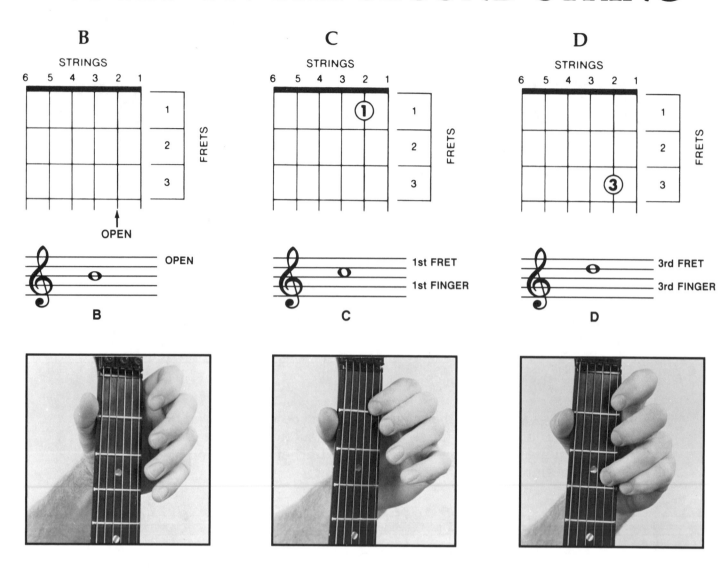

B   C   D

COUNT: 1 - 2 - 3 - 4   1 - 2 - 3 - 4   1 - 2 - 3 - 4   1 - 2 - 3 - 4   1 - 2 - 3 - 4

Hold down 1st finger.

Always practice the exercises slowly and steadily at first. After you can play them well at a slower tempo, gradually increase the speed. If some of your notes are fuzzy or unclear, move your left hand finger slightly until you get a clear sound.

Moving From String To String

You have learned six notes now, three on the first string and three on the second string. In the following exercises you will be moving from string to string. As you are playing one note, look ahead to the next and get your fingers in position.

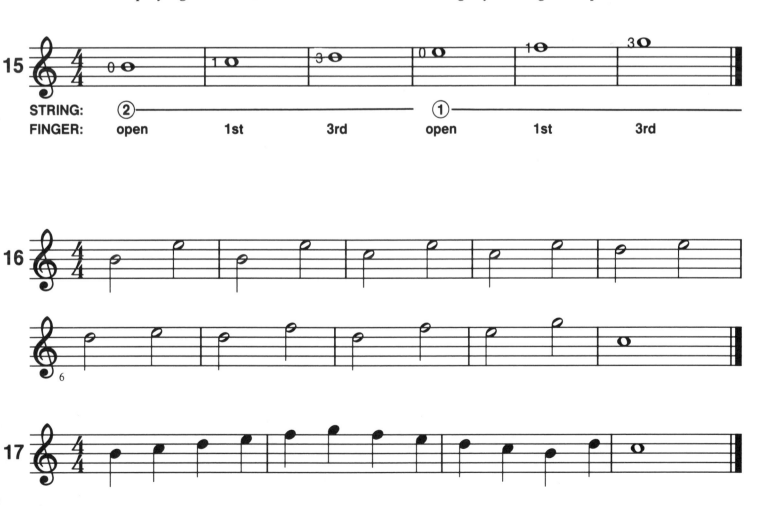

Practice these songs played on strings 1 and 2. Always begin slowly and then gradually increase the tempo. Gray chord symbols are used throughout the book to indicate that the chords should be played by the instructor.

ODE TO JOY ④ ⑤

Beethoven

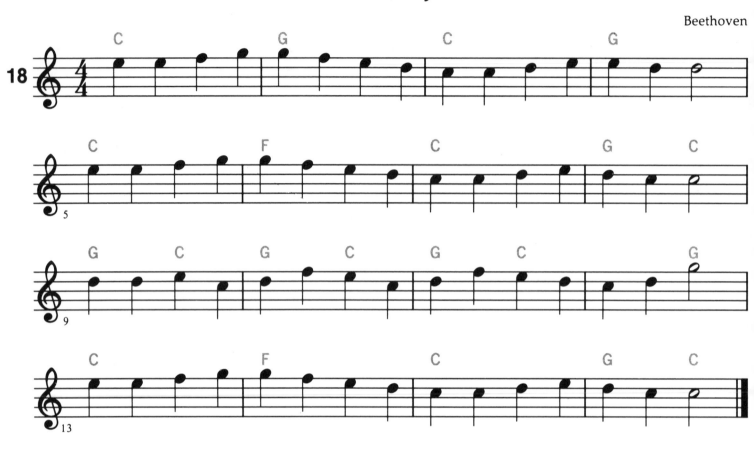

The following piece is a **round** for from 1 to 3 players. Each new player begins when the previous player gets to the asterisk (*). Play it twice through without stopping.

ROUND ⑥

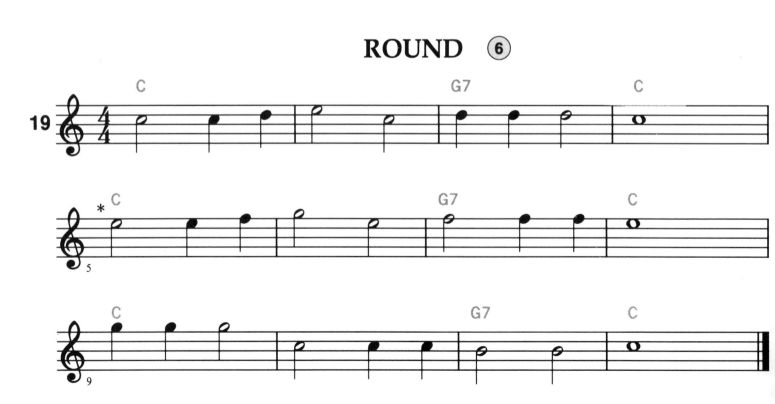

NOTES ON THE THIRD STRING

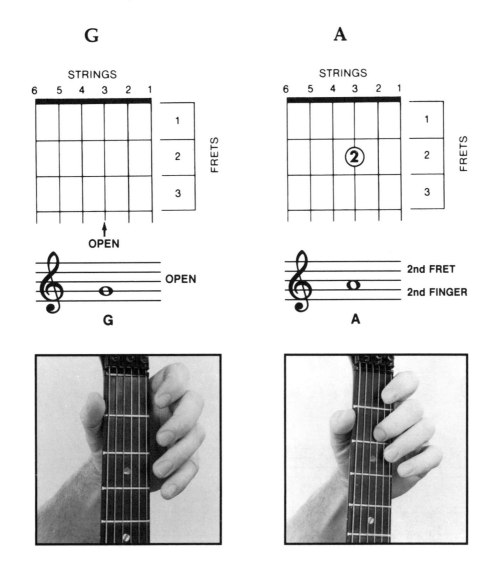

Keep the fingers arched over the strings at all times so they will be in position to finger the next note.

The following exercises and pieces use notes on strings 1, 2 and 3.

22

STRING: ③——— ② ——— ① ——— ② ——— ③

Play for accuracy; then gradually speed up. Use as a finger warm-up.

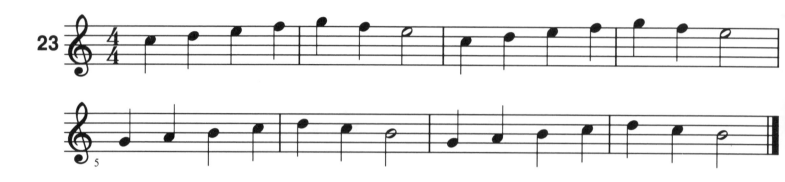

23

YANKEE DOODLE

24

A **duet** is a song that has two parts that can be played together. Practice both parts of the following duet. Ask your instructor or a friend to play the duet with you. If you have a tape recorder, you can record one of the parts and then play a duet with yourself. When you can play both parts, combine them in the optional solo below.

THE BELLS

Duet

Part 1

25

Part 2

Optional Solo

AU CLAIR DE LA LUNE ⑦

France

AURA LEE (8)

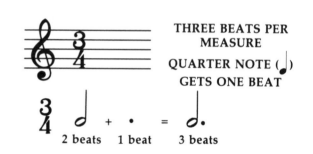

Some music has three beats per measure instead of four. This is indicated by the top number of the time signature. The bottom number (4) tells you that the quarter note gets one beat.

A dot after a note increases its value by one-half. In ¾ time a dotted half note (𝅗𝅥.) gets three beats.

THREE BEATS PER MEASURE
QUARTER NOTE (♩) GETS ONE BEAT

$$\frac{3}{4} \quad \text{𝅗𝅥} \; + \; \cdot \; = \; \text{𝅗𝅥}\cdot$$
2 beats   1 beat   3 beats

COUNT: 1   2   3   1 - 2   3   1   2   3   1 - 2 - 3   1   2 - 3   1 - 2 - 3

HE'S A JOLLY GOOD FELLOW (9)

England

18

3-STRING CHORDS

A chord is sounded when more than one note or string is played at the same time. To begin you will be playing chords on three strings with only one finger depressed.

Strike strings 3, 2 and 1 with a downward motion. All three strings should sound as one, not separately.

C Chord

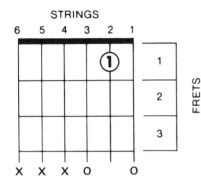

G Chord

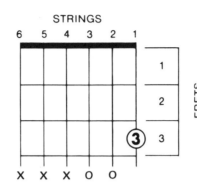

G7 Chord

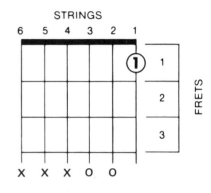

An (o) under a string indicates that the string should be played "OPEN" (not depressed by a finger).

An (x) under a string indicates that the string should not be strummed.

Keep a steady beat, and change chord fingerings quickly.

The chords above are partial chords. If you are ready to learn the full versions of these chords, turn to the **Chord Chart** on page 51.

GUITAR SOLOS

You have been playing either the melody or the chord strums in the previous exercises. Now combine the chords and the melody. First, play through the melodies (the top notes only). When you feel you know the melodies well enough, strum each chord. Finally, combine the melody and the chords. Practice the exercise slowly and steadily and gradually increase the tempo as you progress.

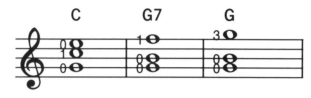

MARIANNE 🔟

Caribbean

All day, all night Mar - i - anne,

Down by the sea - side sift - in' sand.

E - ven lit - tle chil - dren love Mar - i - anne,

Down by the sea - side sift - in' sand.

DOWN IN THE VALLEY

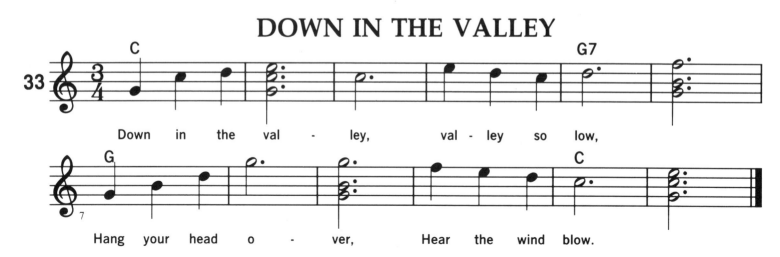

Down in the val - ley, val - ley so low,

Hang your head o - ver, Hear the wind blow.

NOTES ON THE FOURTH STRING

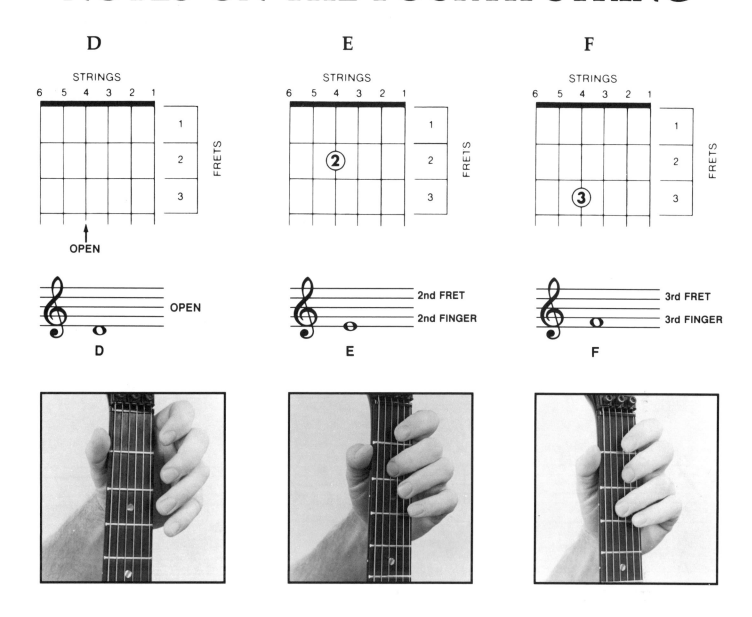

Practice each exercise carefully. Remember to keep your fingers arched over the strings.

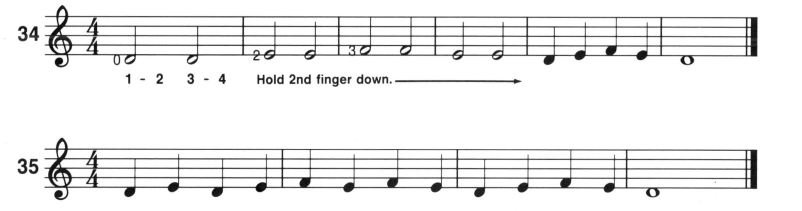

Pickup Notes

Music doesn't always begin on beat one. When you begin after beat one, the notes before the first full measure are called pickup notes. the following illustrations show several examples of pickup notes. Count the missing beats out loud before you begin playing.

THE RIDDLE SONG ⑪ ⑫

When a song begins with pickup notes, the last measure will be short the exact number of beats used as pickups.

Practice playing both the notes and then the chord strums as a duet with your teacher, a friend or a tape recorder.

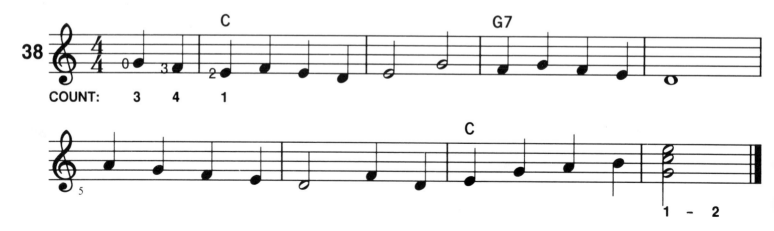

THE D7 CHORD

The D7 chord is a triangular formation of the fingers. You can play the full version of this chord right away. Arch your fingers so that the tips touch only one string each. Strum strings 4 through 1 for D7.

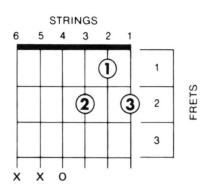

Strum once for each slash mark below.

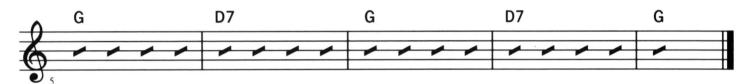

Review the fingering for the C chord and then practice Exercise 40 until you can play it well. Whenever you are moving between the C chord and the D7 chord, keep the first finger down.

12-BAR BLUES-ROCK ⑬ ⑭

Trade off strumming the chords and playing the melody with your teacher or a friend.

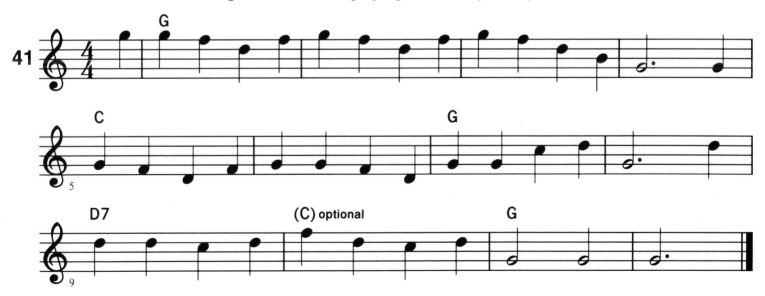

WORRIED MAN BLUES ⑮ ⑯

I takes a wor - ried man to sing a wor - ried song, It
takes a wor - ried man to sing a wor - ried song, It
takes a wor - ried man to sing a wor - ried song, I'm wor - ried
now, yes now, but I won't be wor - ried long.

Ties

A curved line which connects two notes of the same pitch is called a tie. The first note is struck and held for the value of both notes. The second note should not be played again. Look at the following illustration of tied notes.

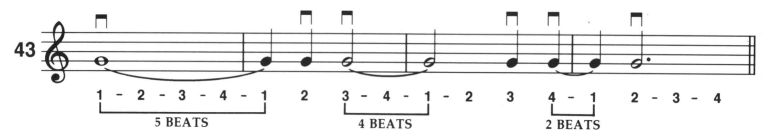

1 - 2 - 3 - 4 - 1   2   3 - 4 - 1 - 2   3   4 - 1   2 - 3 - 4
5 BEATS   4 BEATS   2 BEATS

AMAZING GRACE ⑰

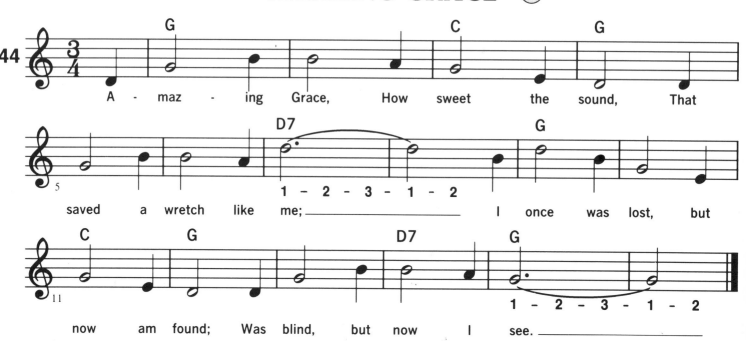

A - maz - ing Grace, How sweet the sound, That
saved a wretch like me; _____ I once was lost, but
1 - 2 - 3 - 1 - 2
now am found; Was blind, but now I see. _____
1 - 2 - 3 - 1 - 2

WHEN THE SAINTS GO MARCHING IN ⓲ ⓳

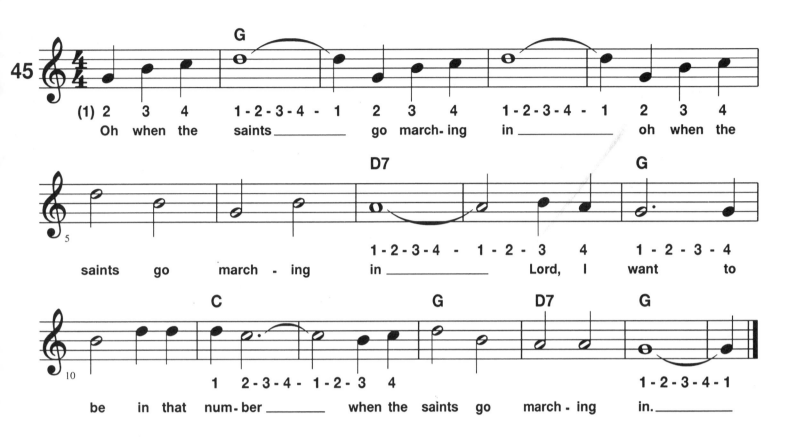

Remember that the chord letters shown in grey are to be played by your teacher.
You should play the melody only on this piece.

THE GYPSY GUITAR

NOTES ON THE FIFTH STRING

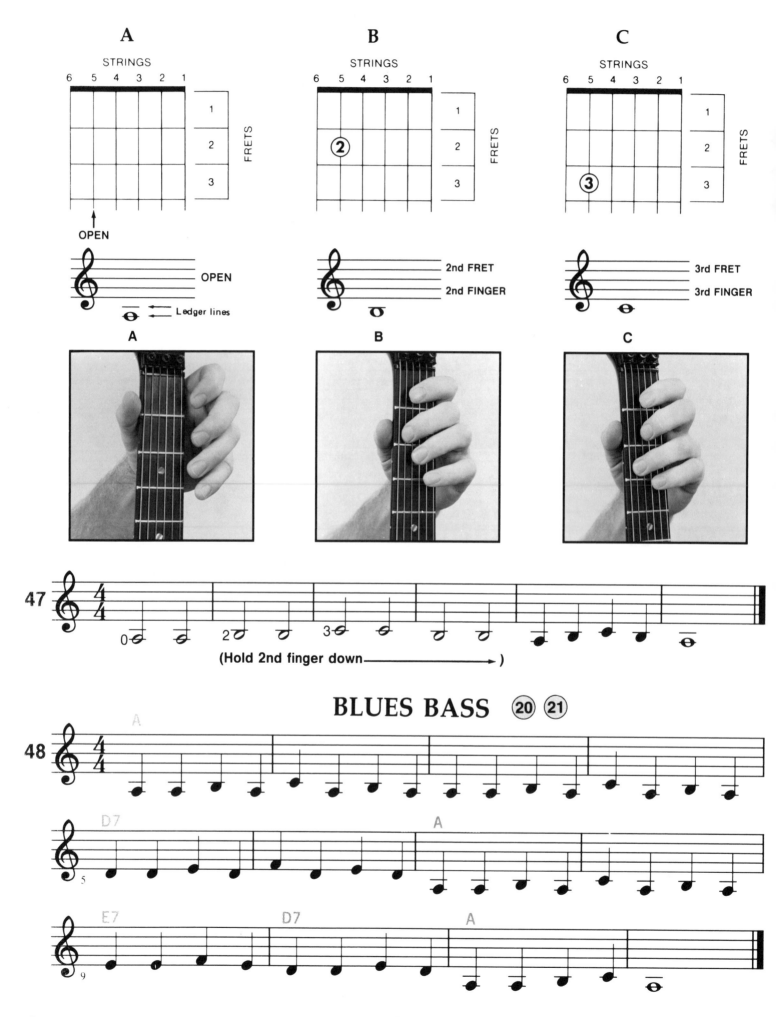

BLUES BASS 20 21

Practice these familiar melodies until you feel comfortable playing them. Remember to look ahead as you play so you can prepare for the next notes.

THE VOLGA BOATMAN

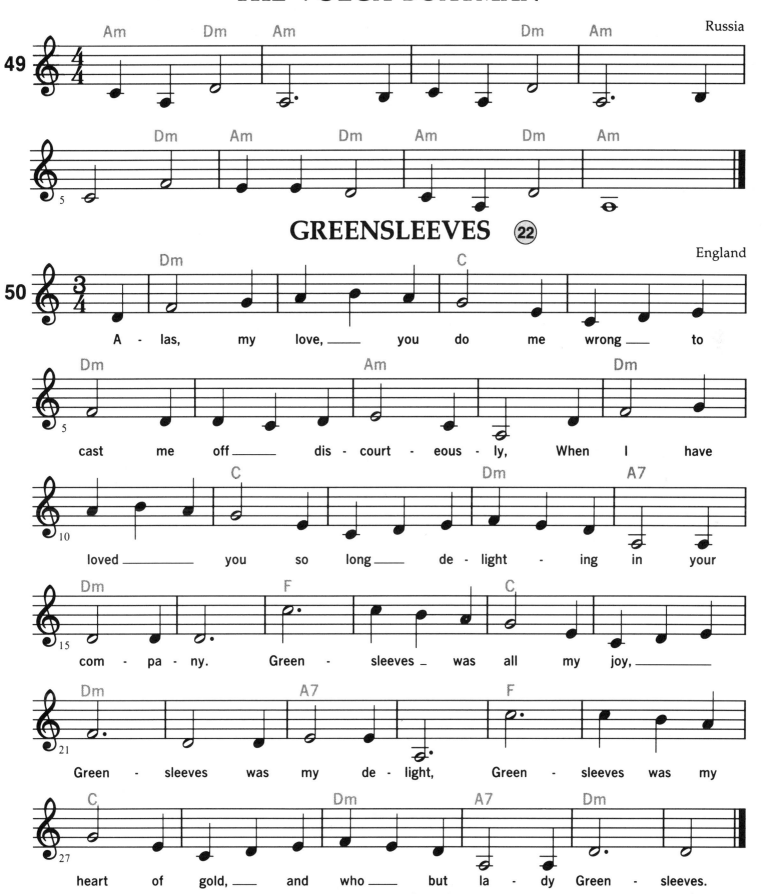

GREENSLEEVES

A - las, my love, _____ you do me wrong ____ to cast me off ____ dis - court - eous - ly, When I have loved _____ you so long ___ de - light - ing in your com - pa - ny. Green - sleeves _ was all my joy, _____ Green - sleeves was my de - light, Green - sleeves was my heart of gold, ___ and who ___ but la - dy Green - sleeves.

NOTES ON THE SIXTH STRING

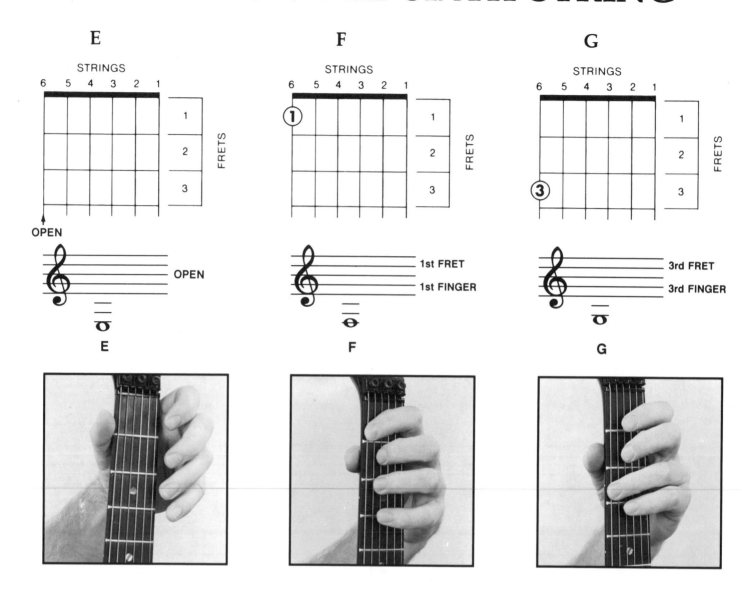

After you play these exercises, write the letter names below each note.

Hold 1st finger down. ──────────►

JOHNNY HAS GONE FOR A SOLDIER

Ireland

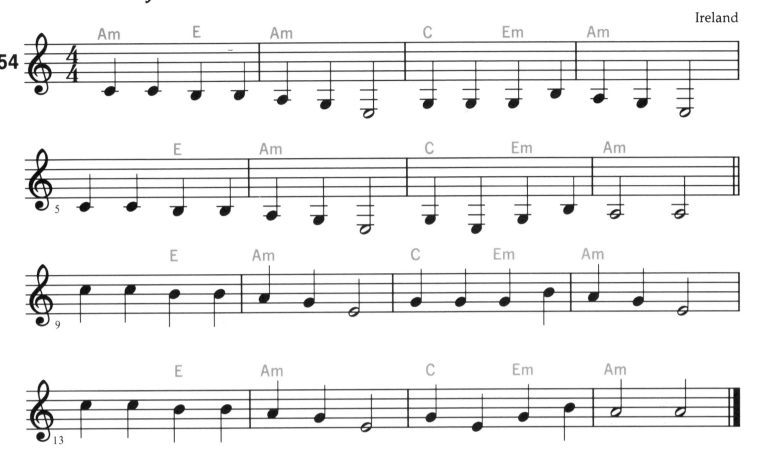

The interval between notes that have the same letter name and are eight notes apart is called an **octave**. The second half of **Johnny Has Gone for a Soldier** is written one octave higher than the first half.

Octaves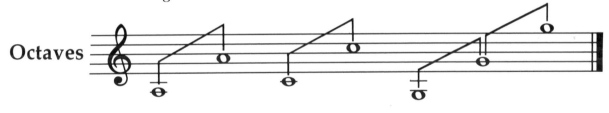

BASS ROCK

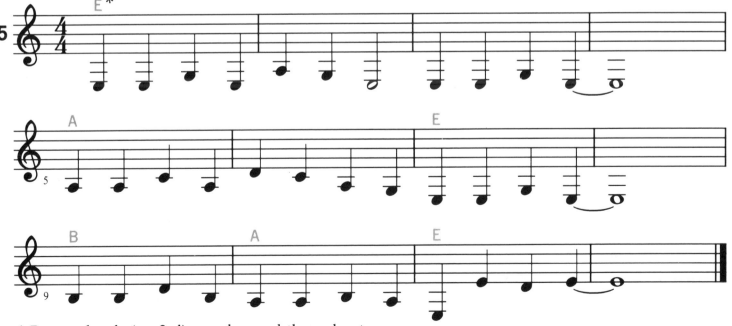

* Power chords (no 3rd) may be used throughout.

Half and Whole Steps

The distance between music tones is measured by half-steps and whole-steps. On your guitar the distance between one fret and the next fret is one half-step. The distance from one fret to the second fret in either direction is called a whole-step.

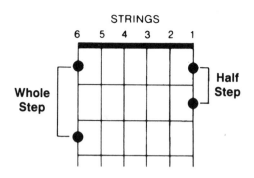

F-Sharp (F♯)

When a **sharp**(♯) is placed in front of a note, the note is raised one half-step and played one fret higher. A sharp placed before a note affects all notes on the same line or space that follow in that measure. Following are the three F♯s that appear on the fretboard to the right:

3 F♯s

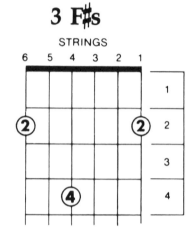

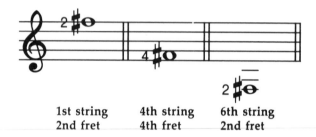

1st string 2nd fret   4th string 4th fret   6th string 2nd fret

Practice each of these finger exercises many times.

LONDONDERRY AIR ㉔

Ireland

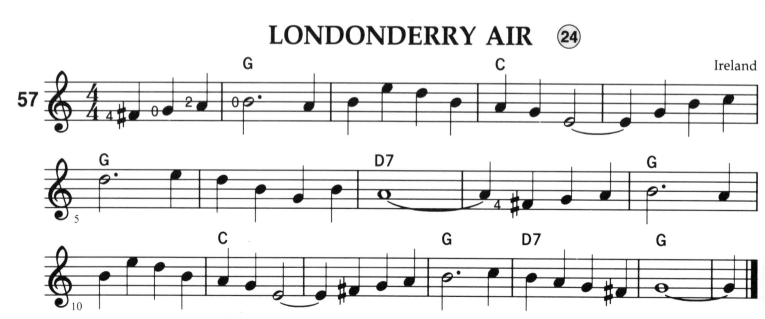

Key Signatures

Instead of writing a sharp sign before every F in a song, one sharp is placed at the beginning of the line. This is called a key signature and indicates that every F in the song should be played as F♯. In **Shenandoah** there will be an arrow above each F♯ to remind you to play F♯.

Shenandoah is written for 1, 2 or 3 guitar parts. Part 1 (the melody) will demand that you count out the tied notes accurately. Use a metronome or tap your foot and count aloud at first. With your teacher, other friends, or a tape recorder, play part 2 and the chords.

SHENANDOAH ㉕

Sea Shanty

Rests

Musical **rests** are moments of silence in music. Each type of note has a matching rest which has the same name and receives the same number of counts.

Whole	Half	Quarter
4 beats	2 beats	1 beat

A rest often requires that you stop the sound of your guitar strings with your right hand as is shown in the photo to the right. This process is called **dampening** the strings. Use the edge of your right hand to touch the strings, and work for a quiet economy of motion with little unnecessary movement.

As you play the following exercises that contain both notes and rests, count aloud using **numbers for the notes** and say the word, **"Rest,"** for each beat of silence.

59

COUNT: 1   2   3   Rest   1   Rest   3   Rest   Rest   2   3   4   1 - 2   Rest   Rest

The letter **R** is used in place of the word, "Rest."

60

1   2   R   R   R   2   3   4   R   R   R   R   1   R   3   4   1 - 2 - 3   R

61

1   R   R   4   1 - 2   R   R   1   2   3 - 4   1   R   R   R

In $\frac{3}{4}$ a complete measure of rest (3 counts) is written as a whole rest (━).

62

1   2   R   1   R   R   1 - 2 - 3   R   R   R   1   R   3   1 - 2   R

ROCK 'N' REST ㉖

Count rests aloud:

JACK STUART ㉗

Scottish

THE FULL C, G and G7 CHORDS

When you began playing the C chord and the G7 chord, you used only three strings. You can play these chords on more strings and the sound will be much fuller. Study the illustrations below for the five-string C chord and the six-string G7 chord. Place each finger in the position shown and strum the chord several times.

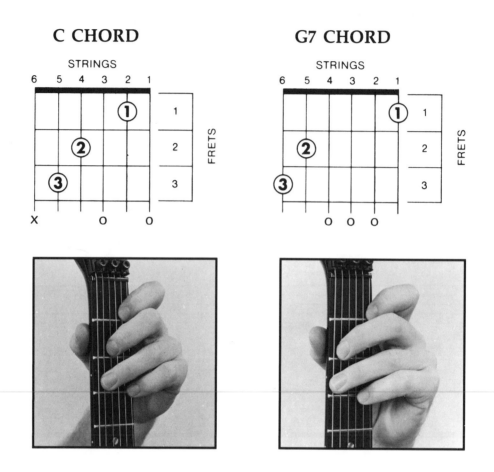

C CHORD   **G7 CHORD**

A double bar with two dots ⁝‖ is a **repeat sign**, and it tells you to play the music a second time.

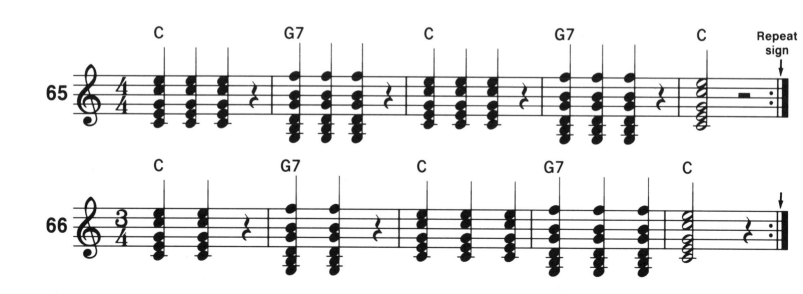

Earlier in the book you learned to play a three-string G chord. Now try the full six-string G chord for a fuller sound. Study the illustrations for the correct finger position. The formation using fingers 2, 3, and 4 will seem more difficult at first, but it will be easier to move to the C chord or the G7 chord. If your hand is small, use the formation with fingers 1, 2, and 3 or the G chord you learned earlier.

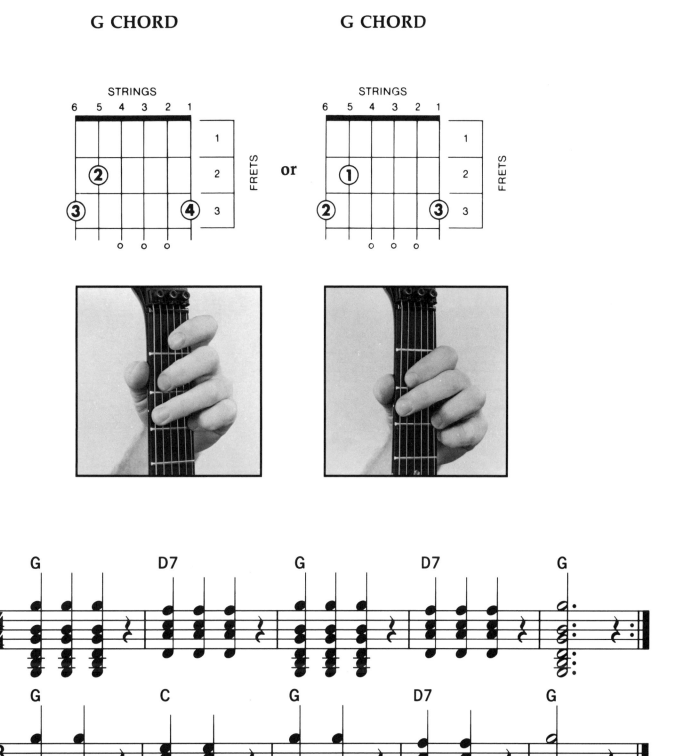

When you can play exercises 67 and 68 clearly and evenly, replace the rests with another strummed chord.

Practice trading off on melody and chords in these pieces.

WILL THE CIRCLE BE UNBROKEN

Country gospel

CORINNA 29

Blues

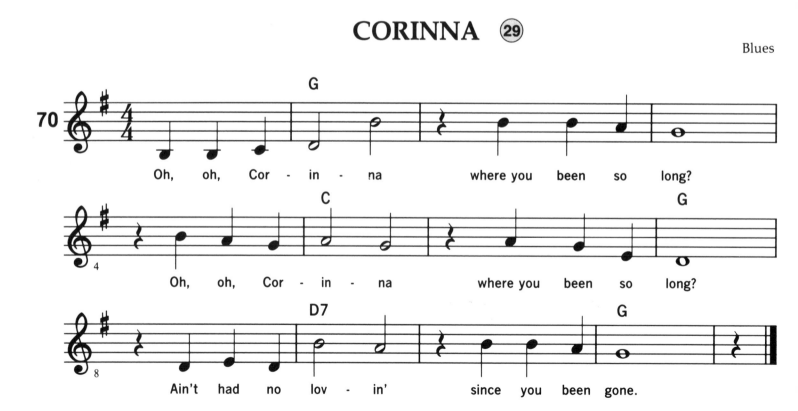

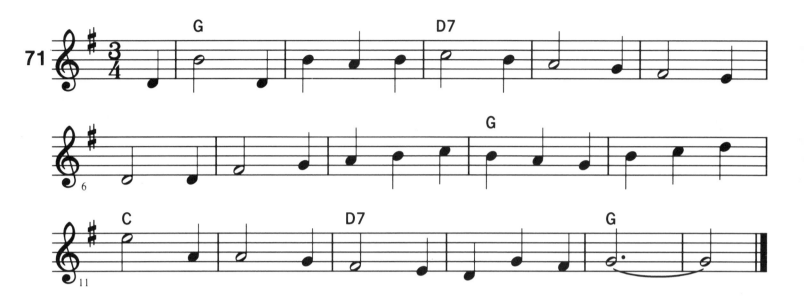

The Bass Note/Strum

When you played chords before, you strummed one chord for each beat in the measure. You can vary the strumming by alternating between a **bass note** (usually the **lowest note** of a chord and the **name** of the chord) and the **remainder of the chord**.

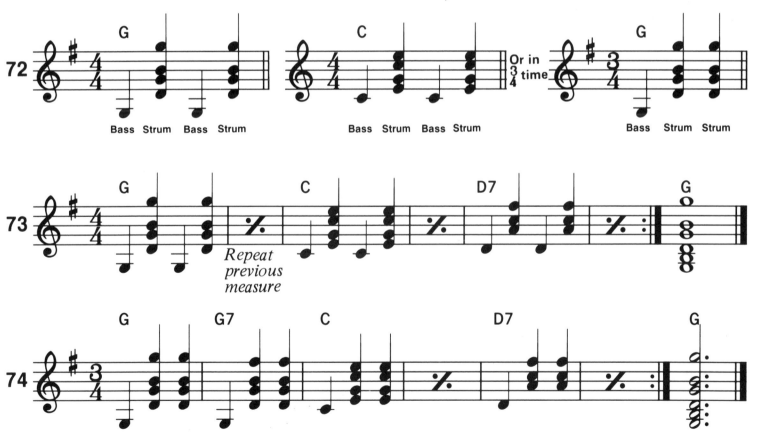

When you can play the bass-strum patterns with a steady rhythm, use them to accompany the previous songs or other songs you already know.

EIGHTH NOTES

An **eighth note** is half the length of a quarter note and gets ½ beat in $\frac{4}{4}$ or $\frac{3}{4}$.

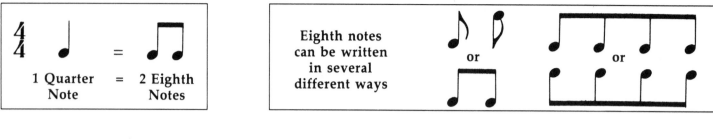

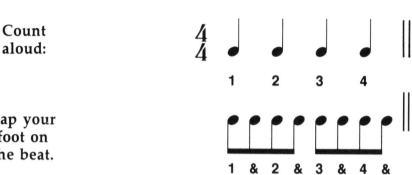

Count aloud:

Tap your foot on the beat.

1 & 2 & 3 & 4 &
(and)

Eighth notes are played with a **down (⊓) stroke** of the pick on the beat and an **up (∨) stroke** on the and (&).

Practice Exercise 76 with an alternating down and upstroke for all eighth notes and a down stroke for all quarter notes. It may help if you think that your pick is tied to your toe. When you tap your foot on the beat, the pick goes down. When your foot goes up on "and," your pick goes up.

Always practice slowly and steadily at first; then gradually increase the speed.

TIRED SAILOR (31)

Sea Shanty

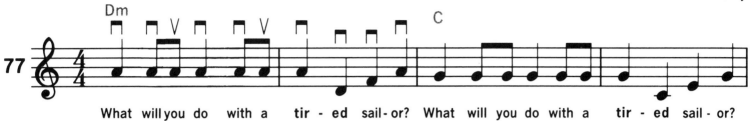

What will you do with a tir - ed sail-or? What will you do with a tir - ed sail-or?

What will you do with a tir - ed sail - or, ear - ly in the morn - ing?

FRERE JACQUES

France

Frè - re Jac - ques, frè - re Jac - ques, Dor - mez vous? dor - mez vous?
Are you sleep - ing? Are you sleep - ing? Broth - er John, Broth - er John,

Son - nez les ma - tin - es, son - nez les ma - tin - es, Din, din, don; din, din, don.
Morn - ing bells are ring - ing, Morn - ing bells are ring - ing, ding, dong, ding; ding,dong,ding.

* **Frere Jacques** can be played as a round. Enter when 1st player reaches the asterisk (*).

SAILORS HORNPIPE

Always check the key signature before you begin. All F's should be played F♯ in BOOGIE BASS.

BOOGIE BASS ㉜ ㉝

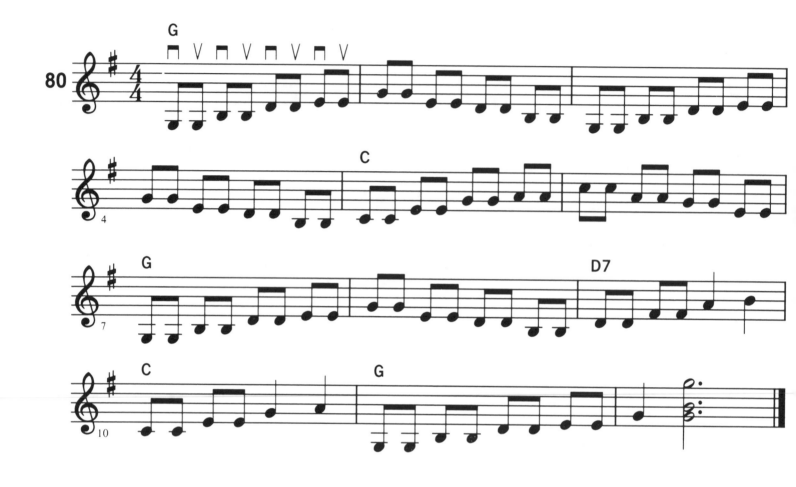

3-PART ROUND

THE E MINOR CHORD

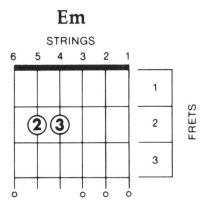

You've played the chords you learned in a variety of ways—as the full chord or only partial chords. The E minor chord can be played the same way. Study and play the example which shows the full six-string chord and a three-string partial chord.

When you are playing the E minor chord in the alternating bass note-chord pattern, use the sixth string for the bass note and the partial three-string chord. Practice the example until you can play it easily and clearly.

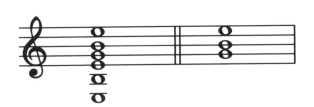

(6th string)

HEY, HO, NOBODY HOME

England

82

Hey, ho, no - bod - y home, Meat, nor drink, nor mon - ey have I none, Yet will I be mer - - - ry

SHALOM CHAVERIM

Israel

83

Sha - lom, cha - ve - rim! Sha - lom, cha - ve - rim! Sha - lom, sha - lom! Le - hit - ra - ot, le - hit - ra - ot, Sha - lom, sha - lom.

*Play as a round if you wish.

Whenever two chords have a common finger position (one or more fingers stay in the same place), you should keep the common finger on the string. In the following progression there is a common finger between the G and Em chord and a common finger between the C and D7 chord. Practice the example until you can play it steadily and without any hesitation between chord changes.

Practice trading off on the melody and chords on **Molly Molone**. When you can play the chords easily, try a bass note with two after-strums that you learned in exercise number 74.

MOLLY MALONE ③④

Ireland

MORE ADVANCED STRUMS

The down-up stroke pattern you have already played on eighth notes can also be applied to strums. As you practice strumming the following exercises, keep your wrist relaxed and flexible. The down-up motion will be much faster and easier if you use down-up motion of the wrist only rather than of the entire arm. This wrist motion feels a little like shaking water off the hand.

BASIC DOWN-UP STRUM

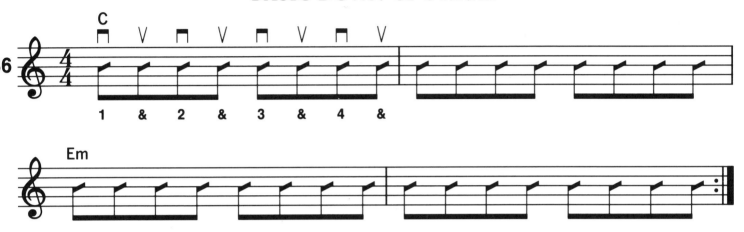

STRUM VARIATIONS

A variation of the basic down-up strum misses the upstroke or "and" of the first beat. Remember to keep the down-up motion going and miss the strings on the "and" of beat one.

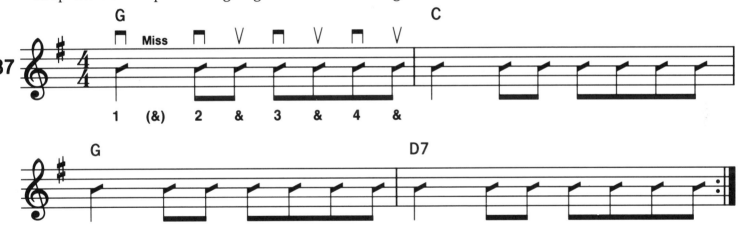

This variation misses two up strokes. Continue to strum but miss the strings on the "and" of beats one and three.

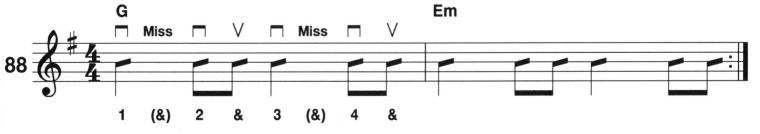

On "Simple Gifts" you can play the melody (Part 1), the harmony line (Part 2), or the chordal accompaniment.

Practice these strums before playing "Simple Gifts."

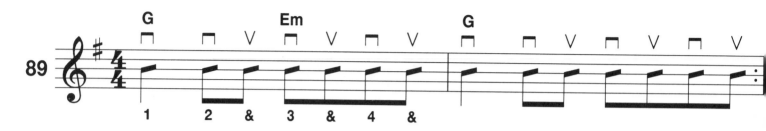

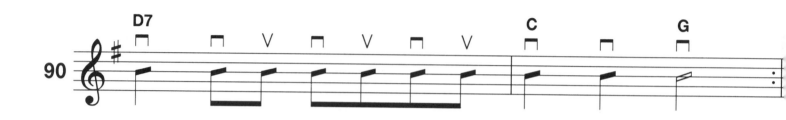

SIMPLE GIFTS 35 36

Shaker song

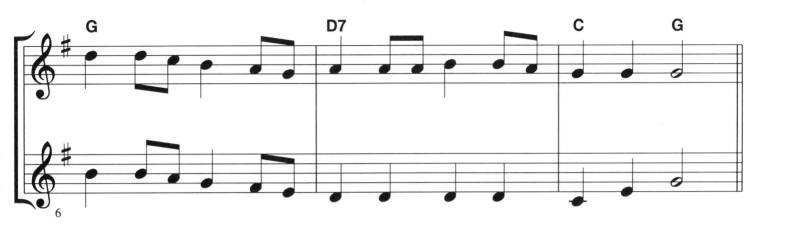

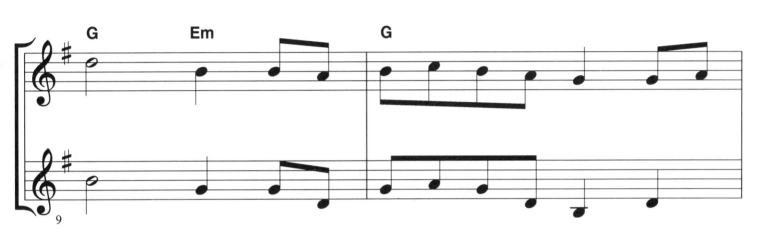

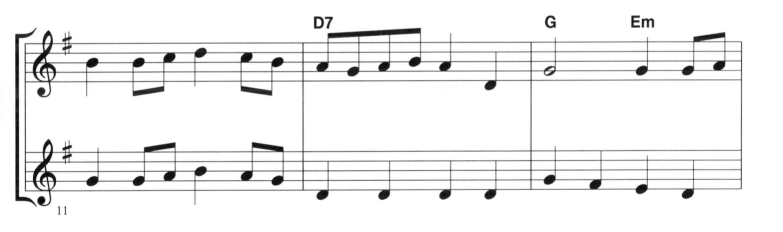

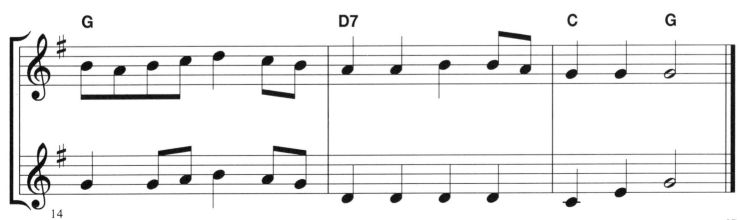

BASS-MELODY SOLOS

This style solo was developed on the Carter family recordings. The melody is played in the bass and long notes (𝅗𝅥 𝅗𝅥. or 𝅝) are filled in with strums. Emphasize the bass melody notes and play lightly on the strums.

ROW, ROW, ROW YOUR BOAT

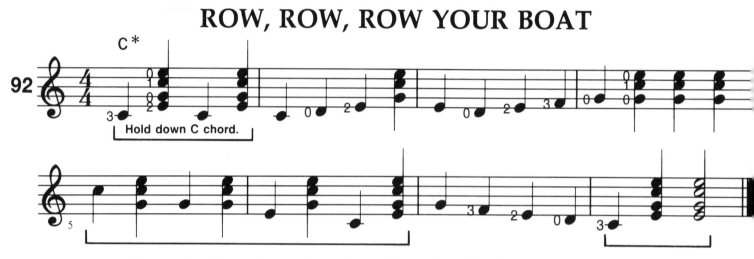

Hold down C chord.

*You can hold your 1st finger down throughout the entire solo if you wish.

WORRIED MAN BLUES ㊲ ㊳

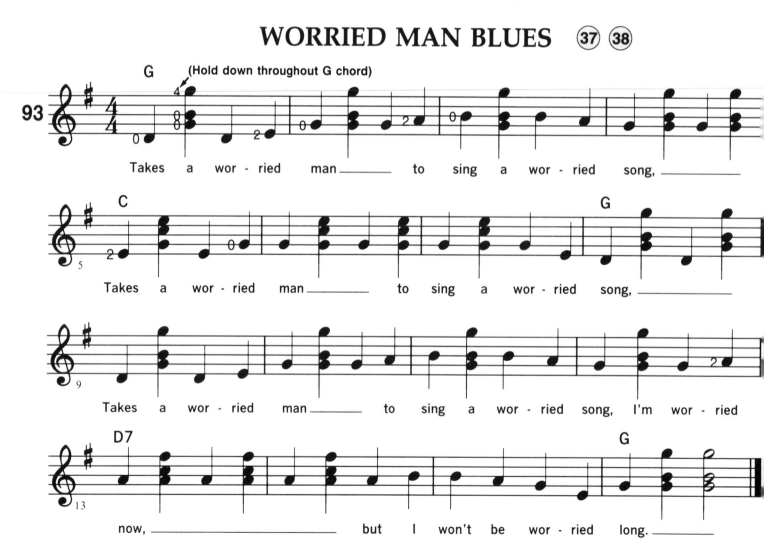

Takes a wor - ried man _____ to sing a wor - ried song, _____

Takes a wor - ried man _____ to sing a wor - ried song, _____

Takes a wor - ried man _____ to sing a wor - ried song, I'm wor - ried

now, _____ but I won't be wor - ried long. _____

WHEN THE SAINTS GO MARCHING IN

94

Oh when the saints _____ go march-ing in _____ oh when the

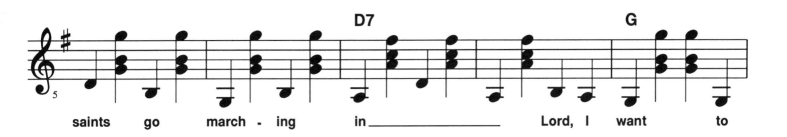

saints go march - ing in _____ Lord, I want to

be in that num-ber when the saints go march - ing in.

When you feel that these solos are coming along well, you might wish to try a variation on the strums. Instead of a single down stroke (⌐), play a down-up stroke (⌐ᵛ). Practice this exercise; then put the down-up stroke in the solos.

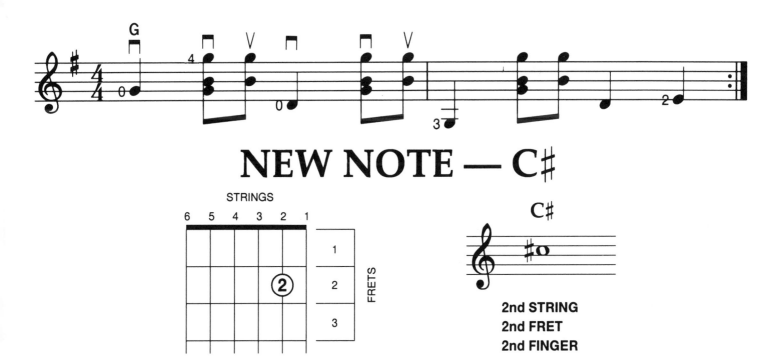

NEW NOTE — C♯

STRINGS

C♯

2nd STRING
2nd FRET
2nd FINGER

MINUET IN G ㊲ ㊵

J.S. BACH
*(Guitar 2 arr.
by W. Schmid)*

95

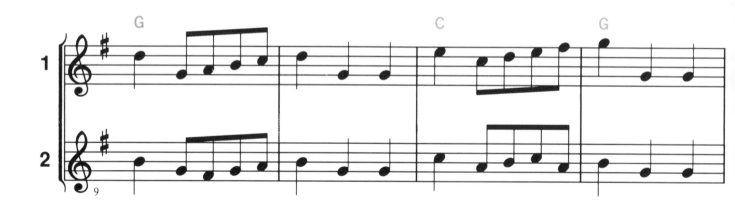

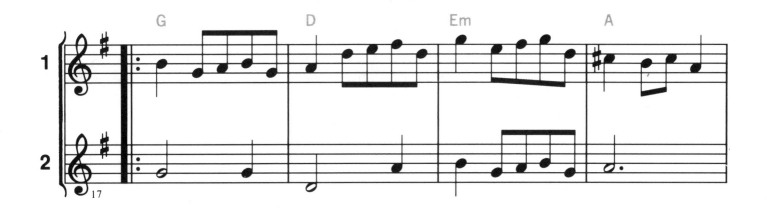

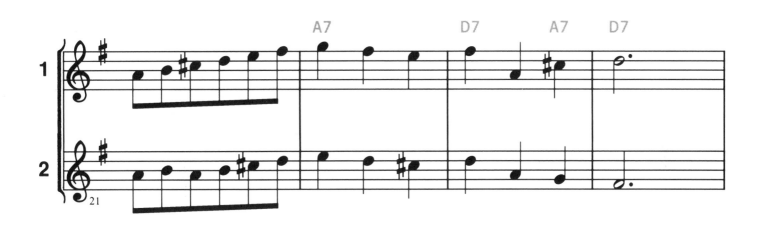

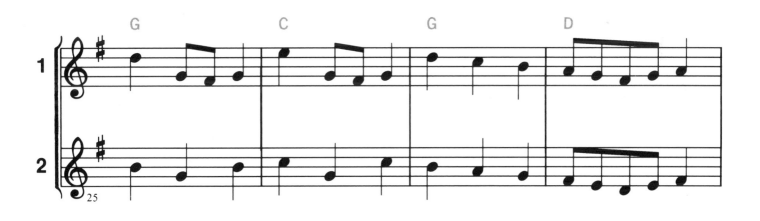

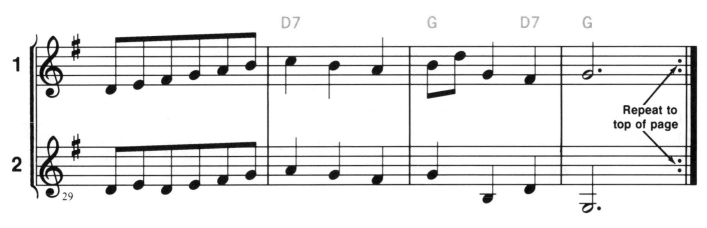

Repeat to top of page

GUITAR ENSEMBLE (41)

3-part round

After learning this Russian "Tumba" round, you may wish to play it with two or three other guitarists. Each player begins when the previous player has reached line 3 at the asterisk. A more advanced player such as your teacher may play the chords (repeating them throughout). Play the round three times through with gradually accelerating speed.

CHORD CHART

In this chart you will find the chords learned in this book as well as several other common chords you may see in music you are playing.

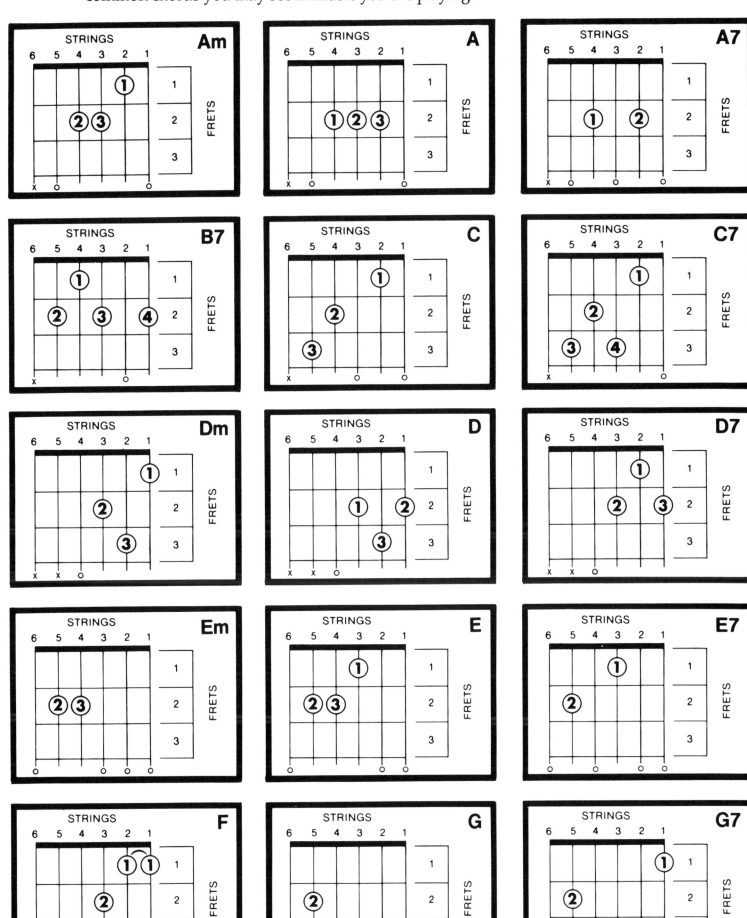

easy POP MELODIES

TEACHER'S AND PLAYER'S NOTE:

This book is a pop, rock supplement to the HAL LEONARD GUITAR METHOD or any other beginning guitar method. Songs are arranged in the same order that notes are introduced in the HAL LEONARD GUITAR METHOD. Chords are given in gray above the melody for the teacher or more advanced students to play.

USING THE CD:

Tune your guitar to the tuning notes at the beginning of the CD. The recorded track for each song begins with one full measure (or a partial measure for pick-up notes) of clicks, which sets the tempo of the song. Songs in a fast speed are first played slower; then fast, so you can learn the notes easier. This is indicated in the upper left corner (slow-fast). On the CD, the *band and melody* are on the left side, and the *band only* is on the right side.

USING THE BOOK:

Tune your guitar following the instructions on page 7. Practice the melody of each song at a steady speed – you may wish to use a metronome or tap your foot. Gradually increase the tempo as you feel comfortable with the notes of the melody. If you have a friend or a teacher who knows the chords (letters above the melody), you can play the songs together. Later when you have learned some of these chords in the CHORD STRUMMER section of the book (page 77), you can come back to this section and play the chord and melody parts on tape or with a friend or teacher.

2 MULL OF KINTYRE

Words and Music by
McCartney-Laine

D.C. (Da Capo) **al Fine** (to the end) tells you to go back to the beginning and play until you reach the Fine.

◆ WHEN I NEED YOU

Words by Carole Bayer Sager
Music by Albert Hammond

Oh, when I need you, I just close my eyes and I'm with you, and all that I saw, want to give you, It's on - ly a heart - beat a - way. _____ Oh, when I need love, I hold out my hands and I touch love, I nev - er knew there was so much love keep - ing me warm night and day, Oh, when I need you.

◆4 ◆5 LET IT BE

slow - fast

Words and Music by John Lennon
and Paul McCartney

When I find my-self in times of trou - ble

Moth - er Ma - ry comes to me Speak - ing words of

wis - dom, let it be. And

in my hour of dark - ness She is stand - ing right in

front of me Speak - ing words of wis - dom, let it

be. Let it be, let it

be, let it be let it be,

Whis - per words of wis - dom, let it be.

⬥ HOUSE OF THE RISING SUN

Traditional

There is a house in New Or -		
I'm go - ing back to New New Or -		

leans, they call the Ris - ing
leans, my race is al - most

Sun. _____ It's been the
run. _____ I'm go - ing

ruin of many poor girls, and
back to end my life be -

I, oh Lord, _____ was one. _____
neath the Ris - ing Sun. _____

BOOK OF LOVE

slow - fast

Words and Music by Warren Davis,
George Malone and Charles Patrick

11 ALL MY LOVING

Words and Music by John Lennon
and Paul McCartney

◆12 SCARBOROUGH FAIR

Traditional English

13 LOVE ME TENDER

Words and Music by
Elvis Presley and Vera Matson

◆14 ◆15 BYE BYE LOVE
slow - fast

Words and Music by Felice Bryant
and Boudleaux Bryant

16 NOWHERE MAN

Words and Music by John Lennon
and Paul McCartney

17 NORWEGIAN WOOD
(THIS BIRD HAS FLOWN)

Words and Music by John Lennon
and Paul McCartney

18 19 EVERY BREATH YOU TAKE

slow - fast

Words and Music by
Sting

20 21 YELLOW SUBMARINE

slow - fast

Words and Music by John Lennon
and Paul McCartney

YOUR SONG

Words and Music by
Elton John and Bernie Taupin

23 24 AT THE HOP

slow - fast

Words and Music by Arthur Singer,
John Madara and David White

🔷25 LOW RIDER

Words and Music by Sylvester Allen, Harold R. Brown,
Morris Dickerson, Jerry Goldstein, Leroy Jordan,
Lee Oskar, Charles W. Miller and Howard Scott

All my friends know the Low Rid - er. The
Low Rid - er drives a lit-tle slow - er.
Low Rid - er knows ev - 'ry street, yeah.
Low Rid - er don't use no gas, now.

Low Rid - er is a lit-tle high - er.
Low Rid - er. He's a real go - er.
Low Rid - er is the one to meet, yeah.
Low - Rid - er don't drive too fast.

Take a lit-tle trip, take a lit-tle trip,

take a lit - tle trip and see. _____
(with me)

MAGGIE MAY

Words and Music by
Rod Stewart and Martin Quittenton

28 IMAGINE

Words and Music by
John Lennon

29 30 THE MASTERPIECE

slow - fast

By J.J. Mouret and Paul Parnes

THE CHORD STRUMMER

USING THE CD:

The CHORD STRUMMER section of the SUPERBOOK was created as a book without a CD. By following the suggestions on page 79, you will not only learn the new chords in this book, but you will learn to combine guitar accompaniments with melodies supplied by singing, humming, whistling, or played by someone else.

FOREWORD

The Chord Strummer is intended for a beginning experience in learning chords, strums and picks for singing and accompaniment. The great collection of contemporary and traditional songs included in this book, combined with the careful development of skills introduced, provide the beginning of a life-long partnership with one of the world's most enjoyable musical instruments — the guitar.

The material presented in this book is only part of the complete spectrum of guitar technique available to you. If, for example, you want to learn more about the instrumental side of the guitar which includes music reading, picking melodies and playing guitar solos, **The Hal Leonard Guitar Method** provides a useful companion to this volume. Later, you will find that other Hal Leonard guitar publications will help further your development of various styles and expand your repertoire of songs. Your development as a player is as limitless as your interest and your willingness to practice.

ACKNOWLEDGMENTS

The author wishes to acknowledge the help provided by thousands of guitar students on whom these ideas have all been tested, hundreds of school and private guitar teachers who have given valuable feedback and the support of colleagues who believe in the experience of studying the guitar and its repertoire.

HOW TO USE THIS BOOK

The sequence of new skills introduced in this book is based on years of teaching beginning guitar students of all ages. If you learn each new skill carefully before going on and keep reviewing the old skills and familiar tunes, your passage through the book should be a smooth one. Nevertheless, there are individual differences from one student to the next: Some learn faster than others, hands come in different sizes making certain chords more or less difficult, and some students find it easier to sing with the guitar. For these reasons, both teachers and students should consider the following guidelines for use of this book.

Learning New Chords
- Study each new chord diagram carefully before playing the chord.

- If there are optional ways to play a chord, begin with the easiest form; then work on the harder form when you are ready for a new challenge.

   Notice that the first chords introduced in the book (C, G7 and G) can be played with one finger or as full three-finger chords. Optional fingers are indicated (p. 80) in light gray. Starting with the one-finger chords is especially helpful to young players, but many adults also start this way. In a guitar class it is common for some to be playing the simplified chords while others are playing the full version.

- After you have learned several new chords, you will find that the challenge comes in moving from one chord to another at the right time.

   Practice the chord exercises until you can do them without looking at your fingers.

   Keep a steady beat and get to the new chord on time (even if you have to leave the old one a bit early).

   Move your left-hand chord fingers as a unit rather than "walking" one finger at a time to the new chord.

Learning New Strums and Finger Picks
- Each time you learn a new right-hand strum or pick, you are calling for new forms of coordination between your two hands (and your voice).

   Practice each new strum or pick until you can turn it on or off like a motor. To test how well you have learned it, try carrying on a conversation with a friend while continuing to play the pattern. This will help you to sing while you play.

- Practice each new strum or pick with any of the chord sequences you know. Always keep a steady beat with your toe or metronome.

- If you are progressing somewhat slower than the rest of the class on right-hand strums or picks, remember that a simpler strum can be used with the more complex ones until you have a chance to learn the new technique.

Learning New Songs
- When learning a new song, always use a simple right-hand strum until you have mastered the left-hand chords. Don't try to do two difficult things at the same time. When you feel comfortable with both the chords and singing, then try a more complex right-hand technique.

- Developing your ability to sing while playing the guitar is a gradual growth process. Make a "joyful noise" and have a good time with it. (My philosophy on singing is pretty well summed up in Bill Staines' great song, "A Place in the Choir" (p. 98).

- The starting note for singing is indicated in the upper left-hand corner of each song in the form of a guitar chord frame. Open-string pitches are given as an(o)above the string to be played. Pluck the string indicated and hum the note before starting.

PLAYING CHORDS

A chord is sounded when more than two notes or strings are played at the same time. To begin you will be playing chords on three strings with only one finger depressed. Disregard the light gray finger numbers on strings 4, 5 and 6 until you can easily play the one-finger versions of the chords below.

An (o) under a string indicates that the string should be played "OPEN" (not depressed by a finger).

An (x) under a string indicates that the string should not be strummed.

The C Chord

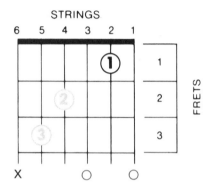

The G7 Chord

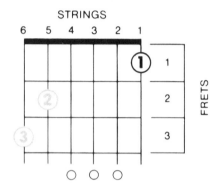

Study the illustration for the one-finger C chord. Do not play fingers 2 and 3 until later when you have mastered the simpler one-finger version. Depress the 2nd string with the tip of your first finger. Arch the finger to avoid touching the 1st string. Strum lightly over strings 3, 2 and 1 with a downward motion of your thumb or pick.

Study the illustration for the one-finger G7 chord. Do not play fingers 2 and 3 until later when you have mastered the simpler one-finger version. Strum across strings 4 through 1 with your thumb or pick.

When the chords are used as accompaniment to singing, they must be strummed with a steady, even stroke. Practice the following exercise strumming once for each chord letter or slash mark (**/**). Repeat this pattern several times.

C / / / / / / / G7 / / / / / / /

Music is arranged into groups of beats or pulses. At the beginning of each song, you will see a number which tells you how many beats are in a group. Tap your foot to help keep a steady beat as you play and sing. Strum once on each beat. Now try this chord exercise with the C and G7 chords arranged in groups of four. Each group of four beats is separated by a vertical line called a **bar line.** Repeat this exercise several times.

4 C / / / | G7 / / / | C / / / | G7 / / / ‖

Now apply this strum to the songs on page 81.

Rock-A-My Soul

Sing:

Rock - a - my soul in the bos - om of Ab - ra - ham,

Rock - a - my soul in the bos - om of Ab - ra - ham,

Rock - a - my soul in the bos - om of Ab - ra - ham,

Oh, rock - a - my soul! _____

He's Got The Whole World In His Hands

Sing:

He's got the whole world__ in His hands,__ He's got the

whole world__ in His hands,__ He's got the whole world__

in His hands,__ He's got the whole world in His hands._____

THE G CHORD

There are several ways to play the G chord. Begin by playing the one-finger version on strings 4 through 1; then add the 5th and 6th string fingers later for the full sound of these chords. The formation using fingers 2, 3 and 4 will seem more difficult at first, but it will be easier to move to the C and G7 chords and will pay dividends later.

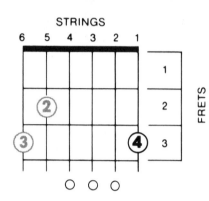 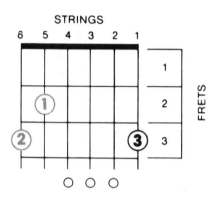

THE D7 CHORD

The D7 chord is a triangular formation of the fingers. You can play the full version of this chord right away. Arch your fingers so that the tips touch only one string each. Strum strings 4 through 1 for D7.

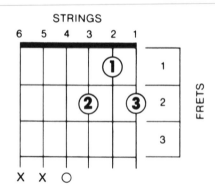

Now play these exercises using the G and D7 chords. The second exercise uses strums grouped in threes.

$$\mathbf{4} \quad \text{G} \; / \; / \; / \; | \; \text{D7} / \; / \; / \; | \; \text{G} \; / \; / \; / \; | \; \text{D7} / \; / \; / \; \|$$

$$\mathbf{3} \quad \text{G} \; / \; / \; | \; \text{D7} / \; / \; | \; \text{G} \; / \; / \; | \; \text{D7} / \; / \; \|$$

You are ready to play **Tom Dooley** in 4-beat groups and **Down In The Valley** in 3-beat groups.

Tom Dooley

Words and Music collected,
adapted and arranged by Frank Warner,
John A. Lomax and Alan Lomax

Sing:

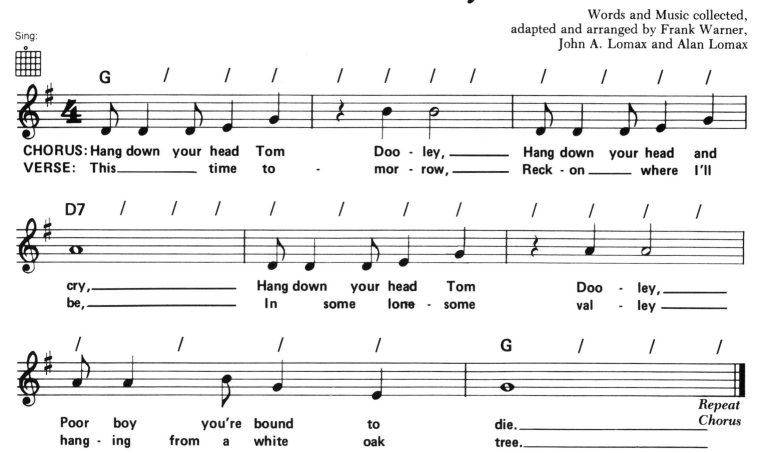

CHORUS: Hang down your head Tom Doo - ley, _____ Hang down your head and
VERSE: This_____ time to - mor - row, _____ Reck - on _____ where I'll

cry, _____ Hang down your head Tom Doo - ley, _____
be, _____ In some lone - some val - ley _____

Poor boy you're bound to die. _____
hang - ing from a white oak tree. _____

Repeat Chorus

Down In The Valley

Sing:

Down in the val - ley, _____ Val - ley so
Hear the wind blow _____ dear, _____ Hear the wind

low, _____ } Hang your head o -
blow, _____

ver, _____ Hear the wind blow. _____

On your first songs, strum marks / were given above the music to guide you in your first stage of development. Once you understand that you should strum with a steady stroke on every beat of the measure, these marks become unnecessary.

The next two songs use the G, C and D7 chords you already know. Strum on each beat of the measure. Keep your right hand steady.

This Little Light Of Mine

This lit-tle light of mine,_____ I'm gon-na let it shine,—

_____ This lit-tle light of mine,_____ I'm gon-na let it shine,-

_____ This lit-tle light of mine,_____ I'm gon-na let it shine,—

___ Let it shine,_ let it shine,_ let it shine._____

        G
2. Everywhere I go, I'm gonna let it shine,
        C   G
    Everywhere I go, I'm gonna let it shine,

    Everywhere I go, I'm gonna let it shine,

                    D7   G
    Let it shine, let it shine, let it shine.

        G
3. We've got the light of freedom, we're gonna let it shine,
        C   G
    We've got the light of freedom, we're gonna let it shine,

    We've got the light of freedom, we're gonna let it shine,

                    D7   G
    Let it shine, let it shine, let it shine.

The song, **Do Lord,** uses this same tune and chords.

Woodie Guthrie's classic song, **This Land Is Your Land,** begins with an incomplete measure — three notes called "pick-up notes." Sing the first three words ("This Land is"); then begin strumming the steady beat where you see the C chord symbol.

This Land Is Your Land

Words and Music by
Woody Guthrie

Sing:

This land is your land, This land is my land,

From Cal - i - for - nia to the New York Is - lands;

From the Red - wood for - ests to the Gulf Stream wa - ter;

This land was made for you and me.

        C   G

1. As I was walking that ribbon of highway

        D7   G

I saw above me that endless skyway;

        C   G

I saw below me that golden valley;

D7   G

This land was made for you and me. *CHORUS*

2. I've roamed and rambled and I followed my footsteps
To the sparkling sands of her diamond deserts;
And all around me a voice was sounding;
This land was made for you and me. *CHORUS*

Go back and learn the full C, G and G7 chords when you feel ready.

STRUM VARIATIONS

Up to this point you have strummed with a downward stroke on each beat of the measure. This simple strum will continue to prove useful on songs where you want an uncomplicated accompaniment.

You can vary this basic strum by adding an UP STROKE after each DOWN STROKE. This DOWN/UP STRUM will seem like it is moving twice as fast, because you will be playing a down/up stroke on each beat.

⊓ is the sign for a down stroke.　　V is the sign for an up stroke.

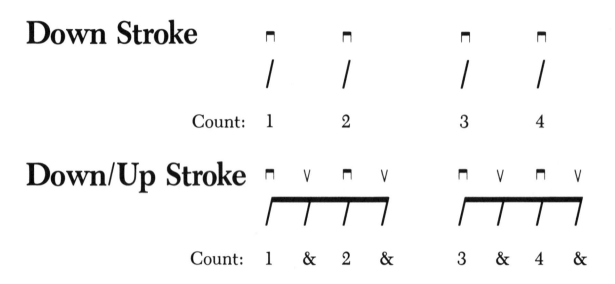

The down/up strum can be played three different ways:

1. A PICK held in the right hand (a louder and "harder" sound)

2. The fleshy right-hand THUMB plays both down and up strokes (a softer sound)

3. The nail of the INDEX FINGER plays the down (brush) stroke, and the nail of the THUMB plays the up stroke. (a harder, louder sound like the pick)
   NOTE: Keep the fingers and thumb relaxed and rotate the wrist. This strum alternates well with finger picking introduced later in the book.

Try all three ways of playing. A good player will use different right-hand strums to achieve different effects for the style of each song.

Play this strumming exercise on the chords you already know:

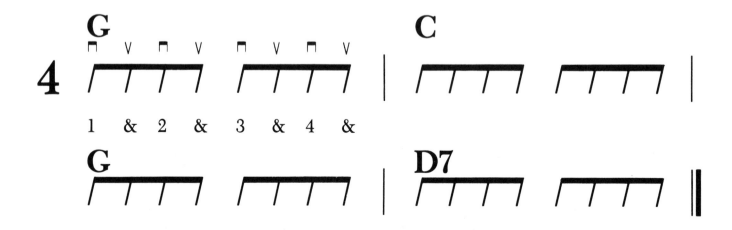

Now play the down/up strum on Elvis Presley's rock hit, **Hound Dog.**

Hound Dog

Words and Music by
Jerry Leiber and Mike Stoller

Keep the common 1st finger down when moving from D7 to C.

Hound Dog is one of many early rock'n'roll hits which uses the form of **12-Bar Blues** borrowed from the black blues tradition. You will return to the blues later in this book on page 117.

If you have not yet learned to play the full G, C and G7 chords, you might wish to return to page 80 and review this material. If you are not ready to play these fuller chords at this time, don't worry; you can always return to these chords at a later point.

THE CAPO

Metal Capo

Elastic Capo

One of the advantages of using a capo is that you can move a song to a vocal range that is comfortable for your voice. The capo also allows you to use easier chords for playing certain songs.

When you use a capo, place it as close to the fret wire as you can. This will help to eliminate string buzzing. If you have considerable warping on your guitar neck, you may find the capo somewhat difficult to use effectively.

On the following page the new song, **Eleanor Rigby,** is pitched in a high singing key where it was sung by the Beatles. The chords are easy to play in this key, so it is written very much like the original version. If you want to sing in a lower, more comfortable key, you can capo at the 5th fret and sing lower. The starting singing pitch is given for use with or without the capo.

THE Em CHORD

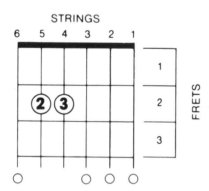

The Em chord is one of the easiest chords on the guitar. Arch your fingers and play on the tips to avoid touching the other open strings.

After you have played through **Eleanor Rigby** using a simple down strum on each beat, try this new variation on the down/up strum:

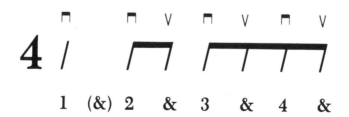

Let the first-beat strum ring for a full beat. Follow the down ⊓ and up ∨ strokes carefully.

Eleanor Rigby

Sing:

Option: Capo 5
and sing lower

Words and Music by
John Lennon and Paul McCartney

Fine

Ah ___ look at all ___ the lone - ly peo - ple! ___

1. E - lea - nor Rig - by, picks up the rice in the church where a wed - ding has been,
2. Fath-er Mc-Ken - zie, writ - ing the words of a ser - mon that no ___ one will hear, ___
3. E - lea - nor Rig - by, died in the church and was bur - ied a - long ___ with her name, ___

lives in a dream. ___ Waits at the win - dow,
no one comes near. ___ Look at him work - ing,
no - bod - y came. ___ Fath - er Mc - ken - zie,

wear-ing the face ___ that she keeps ___ in a jar ___ by the door, ___
darn-ing his socks ___ in the night ___ when there's no - bod - y there, ___
wip -ing the dirt ___ from his hands ___ as he walks ___ from the grave, ___

who is it for? ___
what does he care? ___   All the lone - . ly peo - ple, where
no one was saved. ___

do they all ___ come from? ___   All the lone - ly peo -

D.C. al Fine
after 3rd Verse

- ple, where do they all ___ be - long? ___

Repeat Sign :||

D.C. al Fine

The double bar line with two dots :|| tells you to repeat a section of music. Two repeat signs ||: :|| tell you to repeat the music between them.

"D.C. (Da Capo) al Fine" tells you to go back to the beginning and play until you reach the Fine (end).

89

Tell Ol' Bill and **Where Have All The Flowers Gone?** will give you good practice at combining the Em chord with chords you already know. When you have played the chords to the songs using a simple strum and feel comfortable with your left-hand changes, use the new variation on the down/up strum as an accompaniment.

Tell Ol' Bill

Go back and learn the full C, G and G7 chords as soon as your hand size and progress permit.

Where Have All The Flowers Gone?

Words and Music by
Pete Seeger

2. Where have all the young girls gone? long time passing,
Where have all the young girls gone? long time ago,
Where have all the young girls gone? Gone to young men everyone,
When will they ever learn? When will they ever learn?

3. Where have all the young men gone? long time passing,
Where have all the young men gone? long time ago,
Where have all the young men gone? Gone to soldiers everyone,
When will they ever learn? When will they ever learn?

4. Where have all the soldiers gone? long time passing, (2)
Where have all the soldiers gone? Gone to graveyards, everyone. etc.

5. Where have all the graveyards gone? long time passing, (2)
Where have all the graveyards gone? Gone to flowers, everyone. etc.

THE SYNCOPATED STRUM

Syncopation is defined as off-beat rhythm or the accenting of notes that fall on the & between counts. The syncopated strums so vital to popular music today are a result of the unique blend of African rhythms and European and Latin American musical elements.

Practice the syncopated strums below as a variation on the down/up strum:

- Establish the down/up strum pattern until you can do it without thinking.
- Continue this down/up action throughout the syncopated strums, but "miss" the strings with a silent stroke where you see the word "miss."
- This will result in the desired rhythms and will allow you to easily shift back and forth from one strum to another.

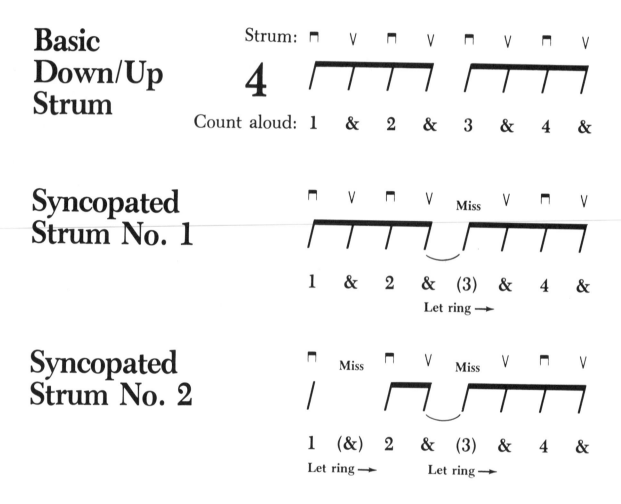

Play the following sequence of chords with each of the syncopated strums above. First, begin with four strum patterns per chord; then decrease the number until you are playing one strum pattern per chord. Tap your foot or play with a metronome to establish a steady rhythm. These strums must be automatic in order to sing with them.

| G | Em | G | D7 |
| G | C | D7 | G |

Before you play the syncopated strums with **The Midnight Special,** go back and apply them to **Hound Dog, Tell Ol' Bill** or **Where Have All The Flowers Gone?**

The Midnight Special

Words and Music by Huddie Ledbetter
Collected and Adapted by
John A. Lomax and Alan Lomax

Sing:

Well you wake up in the morn - ing, _____ hear the ding - dong ring, _____ Go march-ing to the ta - ble, _____ see the same damn thing, Knife and fork are on the ta - ble _____ noth-in' in my pan, _____ And if you say a thing a - bout it, _____ you're in trou-ble with the man.

Chorus

Let the mid - night spe - cial, _____ shine its light on _____ you. _____ Let the mid - night spe - cial shine its ev-er lov-in' light on _____ you. _____

      G   C   G

2.   If you ever go to Houston, you better walk right,

      D7   G

You better not stagger and you better not fight,

      C   G

Or the sheriff will arrest you, he will carry you down.

      D7   G

If the jury finds you guilty, you're penitentiary bound. *CHORUS*

2-BEAT STRUMS

Until now the chords and strums that you have used have all lasted at least four beats or one measure. Sometimes, however, chords change every two beats, and strums that last four beats will not work. At that point, you should switch to a two-beat strum like one of those below:

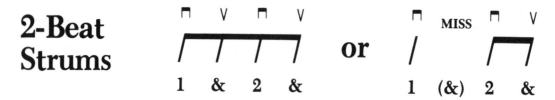

Playing the two-beat strums in isolation is easy, but switching between two- and four-beat strums will take careful practice. Your greatest help will come from maintaining a steady down/up stroke with variations provided by missing the strings with a silent stroke. Practice the following exercises that will help you make the transitions from four beats to two beats:

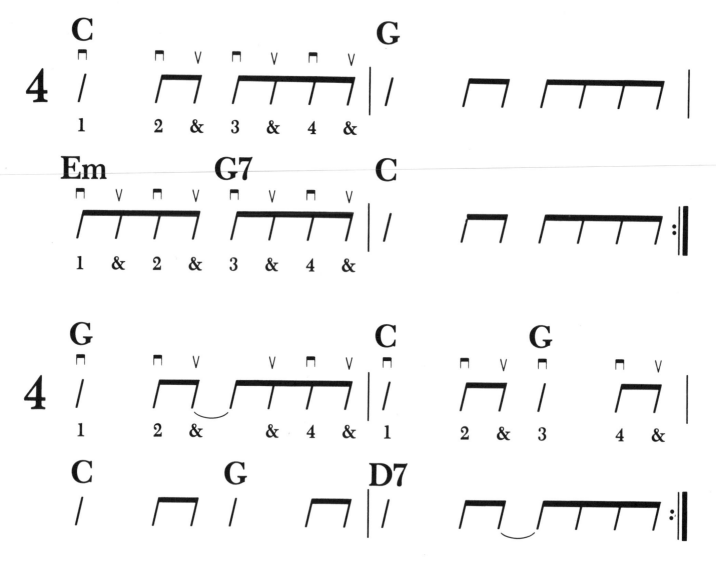

Develop your ability to play the strums with your fingers or with a pick (See page 86.)

Scout your way through **If I Had A Hammer** to find the two-beat chords where your strum must change.

Use a combination of   and   on this piece.

94

If I Had A Hammer

(The Hammer Song)

Words and Music by
Lee Hays and Pete Seeger

Sing:

Option: Capo 3
and sing lower

3. If I had a song, I'd sing it in the morning,
   I'd sing it in the evening all over this land,
   I'd sing out danger, I'd sing out a warning,
   I'd sing about love between my brothers and my sisters,
   All over this land.

4. Well, I've got a hammer, and I've got a bell,
   And I've got a song to sing all over this land,
   It's the hammer of justice, It's the bell of freedom,
   It's the song about love between my brothers and my sisters,
   All over this land.

THE D AND A7 CHORDS

D

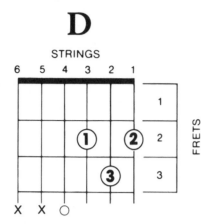

A7

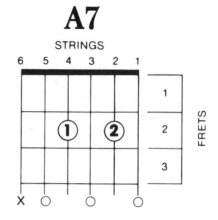

The D chord is a triangular shaped chord pointing toward the body of the guitar. Arch your fingers, and keep your thumb in back of the neck. Play strings 4 through 1.

The A7 chord is easily moved to and from the D chord. Consider fingers 1 and 2 as a unit and move them back and forth together. Arch your fingers so that strings 3 and 1 are not dampened. Play strings 5 through 1.

Practice the following chord changes using any of the four- and two-beat strum patterns you already know. Keep a steady beat with your toe or a metronome. Get to the new chord on time even if it means leaving the old chord a bit early. Try to move your fingers to a new chord as a **unit** instead of "letting your fingers do the walking" one at a time.

4 D / / / | / / / / | A7 / / / | / / / / |

G / / / | A7 / / / | D / / / | / / / / ‖

4 D / / / | A7 / / / | D / A7 / | D / A7 / |

Em / / / | G / A7 / | D / G / | D / / / ‖

Now go back to page 81 and replay the two-chord songs, **Rock-A-My Soul** and **He's Got The Whole World In His Hand**, substituting the D chord for C and the A7 chord for G7. This process is called **transposition**.

Tulsa Time

Words and Music by
Danny Flowers

A Place In The Choir

Words and Music by
Bill Staines

Sing:
Option: Capo 2 or 3

Chorus D

All God's crit-ters got a place in the choir. Some sing low,

D   G   D

some sing high-er, Some sing out loud on the tel-e-phone wire,

A7   D

Some just clap their hands or paws or an-y-thing they got now.____

Verse D

1. Lis-ten to the bass, it's the one on the bot-tom Where the
(2.) dogs____ and the cats____ they____ take up the mid-dle While the

A7   D   G

bull-frog croaks and the hip-po-pot-a-mus Moans and groans with a
hon-ey bee hums and the crick-et fid-dles, The don-key brays and the

D   A7   D

big t'-do, The old cow just goes moo.____ 2. The
po-ny neighs, And the old coy-o-te howls.____ CHORUS

3. Listen to the top where the little birds sing
   On the melodies with the high notes ringing,
   The hoot owl hollers over everything
   And the jaybird disagrees.

4. Singin' in the night time, singin' in the day,
   The little duck quacks, then he's on his way,
   The possum ain't got much to say,
   And the porcupine talks to himself. *CHORUS*

5. It's a simple song of living sung everywhere
   By the ox and the fox and the grizzly bear,
   The grumpy alligator and the hawk above,
   The sly raccoon and the turtle dove. *CHORUS*

THE BASS NOTE/AFTER STRUM

The next stage of development for your right hand is to learn the bass note/after strum technique. The nature of this accompaniment pattern is:

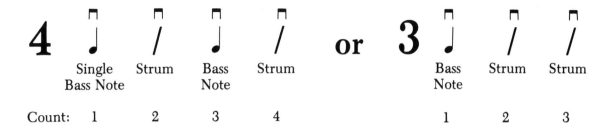

4	♩ Single Bass Note	⊓ Strum	♩ Bass Note	⊓ Strum	or	3	♩ Bass Note	⊓ Strum	⊓ Strum

Count: 1   2   3   4   1   2   3

The bass note/after strum can be played in several different ways:

1. With a **pick** — Play a single bass string; then strum lightly downward across the remaining treble strings.

2. With the **thumb** — Pluck a single bass string with the thumb; then strum downward across the remaining treble strings with the fleshy part of the thumb.

3. With the **thumb and fingers** — Pluck a single bass note with the thumb; then strum downward across the treble strings with the fingernail of the index (and middle) fingers(s).

Playing the proper bass string for each chord will take some practice. Below is a chart showing the correct bass string number for each of the chords you know:

Chords:	A7	C	D or D7	Em	G or G7
Bass String:	5	5	4	6	6

Practice the following bass note/after strum exercise which indicates the string number for each bass note and a slash mark for the after strum:

D   **A7**

4 4 / 4 / | 4 / 4 / | 5 / 5 / | 5 / 5 / |

G   **Em**   **A7**   **D**

6 / 6 / | 6 / 6 / | 5 / 5 / | 4 / 4 / :|

When you can play these patterns with ease, go back to **A Place in the Choir** and **Colours** and apply the bass note/after strum technique to these pieces.

Practice the three-beat exercise below before going on to **Goodnight Irene**:

   D   **D7**   **G**

3 4 / / | 4 / / | 6 / / | 6 / / |

   Em   **A7**   **D**

6 / / | 5 / / | 4 / / | 4 / / :|

Goodnight Irene

Sing:

Option: Capo 2 or 3

Words and Music by
Huddie Ledbetter and John A. Lomax

Chorus

I - rene, good - night,_____ I -
rene, good - night._____ Good - night, I - rene, good -
night, I - rene, I'll see you in my dreams._____

Fine

2. Last
3. Stop

Verse

1. Some - times I live in the coun - try,_____
(2.) Sat - ur - day night I got mar - ried,_____
(3.) ram - blin',_____ stop your gam - blin',_____ Stop

Some - times I live in town._____
Me and my wife set - tled down._____ Now
stay - in' out late at night._____ Go

Some - times I get a great no - tion_____ to
me and my wife_____ are part - ed,_____ Gonna
home to your wife_____ and fam - 'ly,_____ Sit

D.C. al Fine

jump in the riv - er and drown._____
take an - oth - er stroll_____ down town._____
down by the fire - side bright._____

THE Em7 CHORD

The Em7 chord can be played in two different ways — as a subtraction from or an addition to the Em chord you already know. Study the diagrams below:

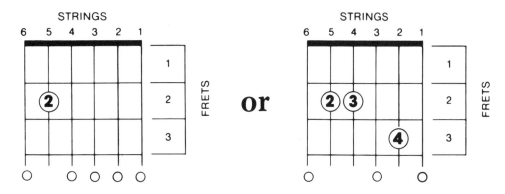

Use either of these strums on **Circles:**

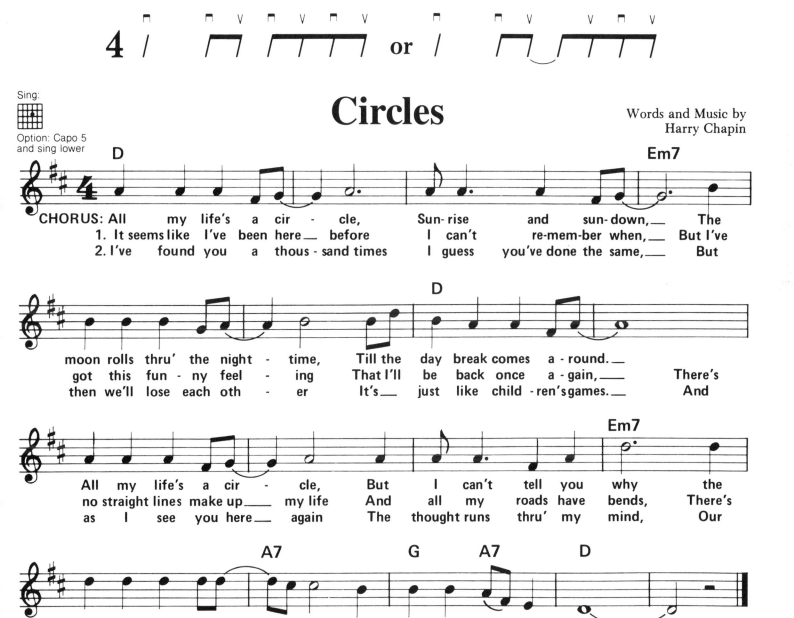

Copyright © 1971 The Harry Chapin Foundation
International Copyright Secured All Rights Reserved

101

THE Am CHORD

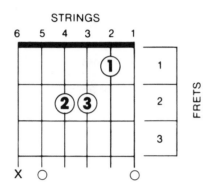

STRINGS

The Am chord should be played from strings 5 through 1. The 5th string should be played as the bass string. Be careful not to lean on the first string and dampen it with your 1st finger.

Play this series of chord changes to become acquainted with Am. First, use any of the strum patterns you already know; then repeat the exercises with the bass note/after strum technique.

Hold down any common fingers between two chords For example, note that the Am and C chords have a common 1st and 2nd finger. Keep these fingers down when changing chords.

4 Am / / / | / / / / | C / / / | / / / / |
Em / / / | G / / / | Am / / / | / / / / :|

4 C / / / | Am / / / | Em / / / | G / / / |
Am / Em / | Am / C / | Am / G / | C / / / :|

Use a simple strum while learning the chords to **Sixteen Tons**; then try the bass note/after strum to accompany your singing.

Sixteen Tons

Words and Music by
Merle Travis

Sing:

Verse   Em

1. Some   peo - ple say a   man   is   made out of mud___   A
2. (I was)   born___ one___   morn - in' when the sun did - n't shine___   I
3. (I was)   born___ one___   morn - in', it was driz - zl - ing rain_____
4. (If you)   see____ me____   com - in' bet - ter___   step a - side___   A

poor   man's   made   out   of   mus - cle and   blood_____
picked up   my   shov - el   and   I   walked to   the   mine, I load - ed
Fight - in' and   trou - ble are_____ my   mid - dle name I   was
lot - ta men   did - n't_____ a   lot - ta men   died_____

Am

Mus - cle and   blood   and   skin   and   bones_____ A
Six - teen Tons   of   num - ber nine   coal And   the
raised_____ in   a   cane - brake by   an   ole   ma - ma lion, Cain't no
One_____ fist   of   i - ron_____ the   oth - er of   steel, If   the

C   **Em**

mind   that's   weak   and   a   back   that's   strong. You   load
straw - boss   said   "Well - a   bless   my   soul." You   load
high - toned wo - man make me   walk   the   line. You   load
right one don't - a get   you, then   the   left   one   will. You   load

Chorus

Six - teen Tons,   what   do   you   get?_____ An -

oth - er day   old - er and   deep - er in   debt._____ Saint

Am

Pe - ter, don't   you   call   me   'cause   I   can't   go_____ I

Em

owe_____ my   soul   to   the   com - pa - ny   store._____

1,2,3   **4**

_____   2. I   was   _____
                 3. I   was
                 4. If you

The symbol ⌒ is called a **fermata**; and it tells you to **hold** a note.

The brackets over the last line are called **endings.** Play the ⌐1, 2, 3————⌐ ending after verses 1, 2 and 3 repeating back to the beginning. On verse 4 skip over the ⌐1, 2, 3————⌐ and play the ⌐4————— ending.

THE Am7 CHORD

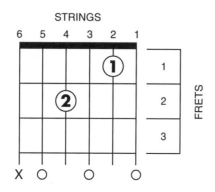

The Am7 chord is a variation on the Am chord by subtracting the 3rd finger. Play a 5th string bass note and strum strings 5 through 1. Be careful not to mix up this chord with A7.

Use either one or a mixture of these strums on **Fire and Rain**:

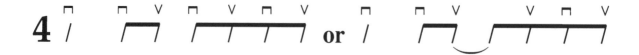

Fire and Rain

Sing:

Words and Music by
James Taylor

104

I just can't re-mem-ber who to send — it to. _____

Chorus

I've seen fire and I've seen rain _____ I've seen

sun-ny days _ that I thought would nev-er end. _____ I've seen

lone-ly times _ when I could not find _ a friend _____ But I

al-ways thought I'd see you a-gain. _____

    D   **Am7**   **G**   **D**
2. Look down upon me, Jesus, you've got to help me make a stand

        A7   **C**
You've got to see me through another day

D   **Am7**   **G** **D**
My body's aching and my time is at hand

        A7   **C**
And I won't make it any other way. *CHORUS*

    D   **Am7**   **G**   **D**
3. Walking my mind to an easy time my back turned towards the sun

        A7   **C**
Lord knows when the cold wind blows it'll turn your head around

        D   **Am7**   **G**   **D**
Well, there's hours of time on the telephone line to talk about things to come

        A7   **C**
Sweet dreams and flying machines in pieces on the ground. *CHORUS*

THE Dm CHORD

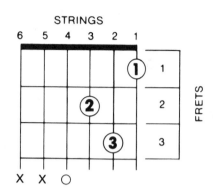

The bass string for the Dm chord is the 4th string. Strum strings 4 through 1.

Use a combination of two different strums on the sea shanty, **The Drunken Sailor:**

Sing:

Drunken Sailor

Verse   Dm   C

1. What will you do with a drunk-en sail-or? What will you do with a drunk-en sail-or?

Dm   Am   Dm

What will you do with a drunk-en sail-or, Ear-lye in the morn-ing?

Chorus   Dm   C

'Way, hey, and up she ris-es, 'Way, hey, and up she ris-es

Dm   Am   Dm

'Way, hey, and up she ris-es ear-lye in the morn-ing.

2. Put him in the brig until he's sober (3) ear-lye in the morning. *CHORUS*

3. Put him in the scuppers with the hosepipe on him (3) *CHORUS*

4. Shave his belly with a rusty razor (3) *CHORUS*

FINGER PICKING

Finger picking is a very popular style of guitar accompaniment which uses **arpeggios** (broken chords) instead of strummed chords. The distinctive sound of finger picking comes from the thumb and fingers plucking only one string each in succession.

The finger and thumb letters used in this book and in all other Hal Leonard guitar books are based on the internationally accepted system of Spanish words and letters:

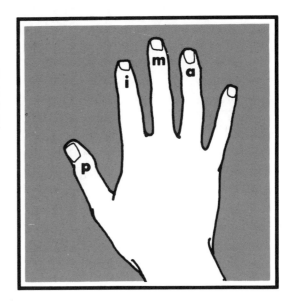

p **pulgar** = thumb

i **indice** = index finger

m **medio** = middle finger

a **anular** = ring finger

Follow these steps to learn how to finger pick:
- The thumb (p) plucks strings 4, 5, or 6 depending upon which string is the bass or root of the chord. This motion is a downward stroke. Use the left side of the thumb and thumbnail.
- The other fingers (i, m, a) pluck the string in an upward stroke with the fleshy tip of the finger and fingernail.
- The index finger (i) always plucks string 3.
- The middle finger (m) always plucks string 2.
- The ring finger (a) always plucks string 1.

The thumb and each finger must pluck only one string per stroke and not brush over several strings. (This would be a strum.) Let the strings ring throughout the duration of the chord.

Right-Hand Position

Use a high wrist; arch your palm as if you were holding a ping-pong ball; keep the thumb outside and away from the fingers; and let the fingers do the work rather than lifting your whole hand.

Keeping in mind the bass string number for each chord (This is the string plucked by the thumb **p**), practice the pattern below: Work toward an even sound on each string plucked. Each line below represents a guitar string. (The numbers are given at the left.)

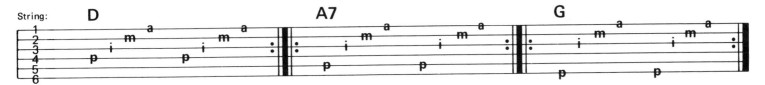

Use the p-i-m-a pattern of finger picking you have just learned as an accompaniment to **The Worried Man Blues.** The pick is indicated under the first line of music to help you see the relationship of one pick per beat to the song above.

The Worried Man Blues

Continue finger pick throughout.

1. **Twenty-nine links of chain around my leg, (3 times)
   And on each link an initial of my name. CHORUS**

2. **I asked the judge, "What might be my fine ?" (3 times)
   "Twenty-one years on the Rocky Mountain Line." CHORUS**

3. **If anyone should ask you "Who made up this song?"
   Say, "Twas I, and I sing it all night long." CHORUS**

When you have thoroughly learned the finger pick written above, try doubling the speed of the right-hand pick so that here are two **p-i-m-a** patterns per measure.

Practice the three-beat finger picking pattern before applying it to **Scarborough Fair.**

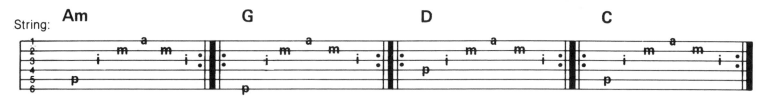

Use a simple strum while you are becoming familiar with the chords to **Scarborough Fair;** then, when you are comfortable with both singing and accompanying yourself, apply the finger pick which is written below the first line of music as a sample.

Scarborough Fair

Traditional

Continue finger pick throughout

Am   G Am   C   Am D   Am
2. Tell her to make me a cambric shirt,_____   Parsley, sage, rosemary and thyme,
       C Am G   Am   D G   Am
Without any seam or needle work,_____   Then she'll be a true love of mine.

THE A CHORD

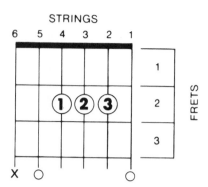

STRINGS

FRETS

The A major chord is a lot like the A7 chord with the space (string 3) filled in. Arch your fingers so the 1st string rings as an open string. The 5th string is the bass note for the A chord.

The following song, **Yellow Submarine**, uses a variation on the basic down/up strum you already know. The difference lies in the uneven rhythm which is used: (This is the same rhythm as "Mine eyes have seen the glory of the coming of the Lord" from the **Battle Hymn of the Republic**.)

Bump - ty   Bump - ty   Bump - ty   Bump - ty

This same rhythm (sometimes called "dotted" rhythm because it uses dotted notes) can be applied to the finger pick, **p-i-m-a**, used twice in each measure. Practice the following chord sequence first with the down/up strum, then with the finger pick:

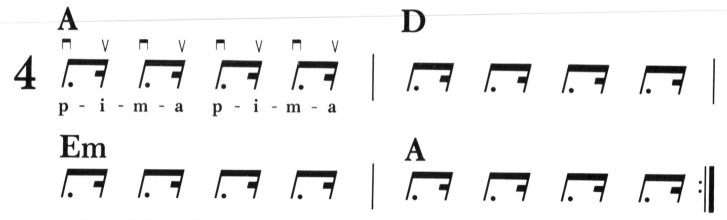

A   D

p - i - m - a   p - i - m - a

Em   A

Learn **Yellow Submarine** with strums; then play the finger pick.

Yellow Submarine

By John Lennon
and Paul McCartney

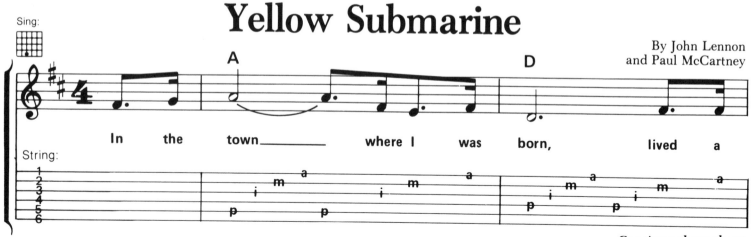

Sing:

In   the   town_____   where I   was   born,   lived   a

String:

Continue throughout.

man _____ who sail'd the sea. _____ And he told _____ us of his

life _____ in the land _____ of sub - ma - rines. So we

sail'd _____ up to the sun _____ 'til we found _____ the sea of

green. _____ And we liv'd _____ be - neath the waves _____ in our

yel - low sub - ma - rine. We all live in a yel - low sub-ma-rine,

yel - low sub - ma-rine, yel - low sub - ma-rine. We all live in a

yel - low sub - ma-rine, yel - low sub - ma-rine, yel - low sub - ma-rine.

THE E CHORD

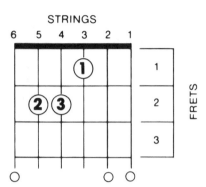

The E chord is played with the same finger formation as the Am chord you know, except that the fingers are moved one string over to strings 3, 4, and 5. The bass note is played on the 6th string.

D.S. al Coda is a musical direction which tells you to go back to the sign 𝄋; then play through the first three lines until you take the 2nd ending; where you see another sign ⊕ which tells you to go to the Coda (the last two lines on page 113). Follow the musical roadmap with your eyes before playing.

Hey Jude

Words and Music by
John Lennon and Paul McCartney

The Rainbow Connection

By Paul Williams
and Kenneth L. Ascher

Sing:

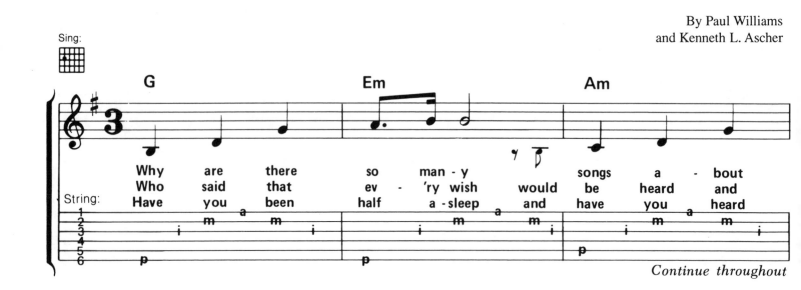

Why are there so man-y songs a-bout
Who said that ev-'ry wish would be heard and
Have you been half a-sleep and have you heard

String:

Continue throughout

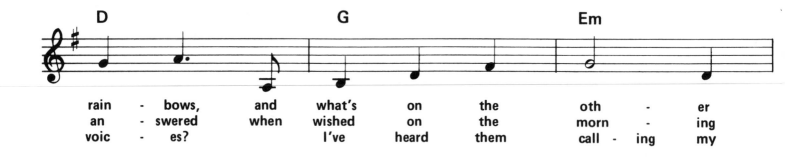

rain - bows, and what's on the oth - er
an - swered when wished on the morn - ing
voic - es? I've heard them call - ing my

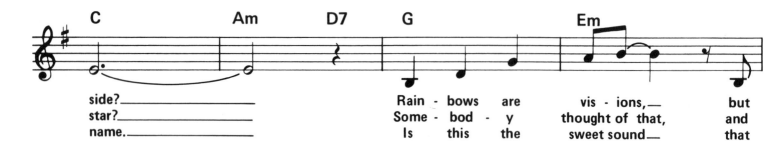

side?_____ Rain - bows are vis - ions,— but
star?_____ Some - bod - y thought of that, and
name._____ Is this the sweet sound— that

on - ly il - lu - sions, And rain - bows have
some - one be - lieved it; Look what it's
calls one the young sail - ors? The voice might be

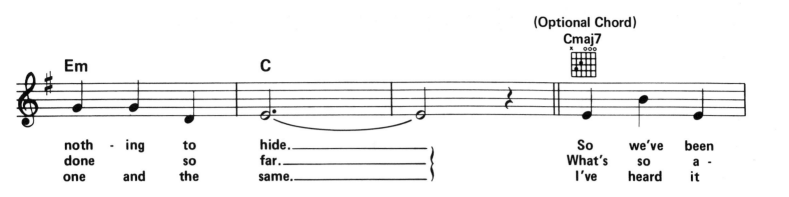

noth - ing to hide._____
done so far._____
one and the same._____

So we've been
What's so a -
I've heard it

told, and some choose to be - lieve it;
maz - ing that keeps us star - gaz - ing And
too man - y times to ig - nore it. It's

(Optional Chord)
Dmaj7 or D

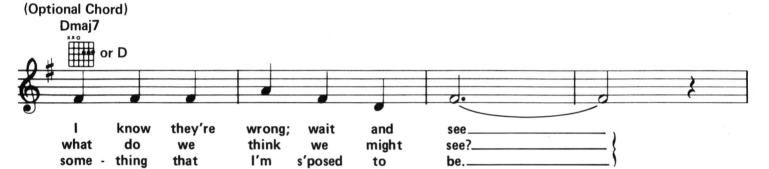

I know they're wrong; wait and see_____
what do we think we might see?_____
some - thing that I'm s'posed to be._____

Some - day we'll find it, the rain - bow con -

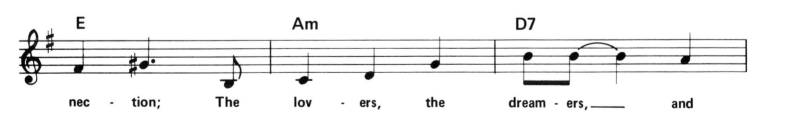

nec - tion; The lov - ers, the dream - ers,_____ and

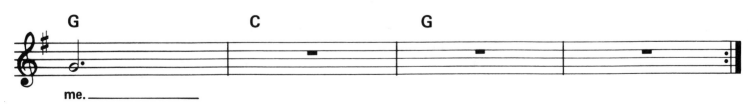

me._____

THE B7 CHORD

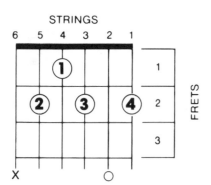

STRINGS

FRETS

B7 is your first four-finger chord. Notice that the 2nd-fret fingers are placed on strings 1, 3 and 5. Keeping this visual pattern in mind will help you move to this chord quickly. When you change from E to B7, keep the 2nd finger down. The bass string for B7 is the 5th string.

Ramblin' Round

Words by Woody Guthrie
Music based on "Goodnight Irene" by
Huddie Ledbetter and John A. Lomax

Chorus: Ram - blin' 'round your cit - y,___ Ram - blin'
Verse 1. Some folks say I'm worth-less,___ Some folks

'round your town._____ I al - ways meet a
say I'm poor._____ But I'm the rich - est

friend I know As I go ram - blin' 'round,
man I know, I could not han - dle more,

boys, As I go ram - blin, 'round._____
boys, I could not han - dle more._____

*Use the bass note/after strum (3 ♩ / /) accompaniment.

2. **Some folks long for silver, Some folks long for gold.**
   But all I want's a life that's free,
   And I will never grow old, boys, And I will never grow old.

3. **(Why not try making up a verse or two of your own?)**

116

THE E7 CHORD

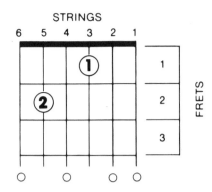

There are two ways of playing the E7 chord — either as a subtraction from or an addition to the E chord you already know. The four-finger version is preferable if you are finger picking. The bass note for E7 is the 6th string.

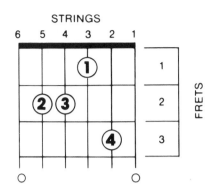

The **12-bar blues** form (12 measures) is one of the most important forms of American music. Notice the three phrases of four measures each and that the first line of text repeats followed by a rhyming line (AAB). After you have thoroughly absorbed the chord progression and the feel of the song, try making up some of your own verses. 12-bar blues became the basis for many early rock 'n' roll hits.

Good Mornin' Blues

2. Lay down last night, tryin' to take my rest, (2 times)
   My mind kept ramblin' like the wild geese in the west.

3. The sun gonna shine on my back door some day. (2 times)
   The wind gonna rise up and blow my blues away.

*Use a down/up strum with a dotted rhythm.

THE F CHORD

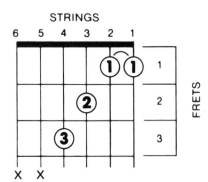

STRINGS

6 5 4 3 2 1

FRETS

Unlike other chords you have played, the F chord has two strings depressed by one finger. The first finger forms a small "bar" across strings 1 and 2. You will find that it is easier to roll this finger slightly so that the strings are depressed by the outside rather than the flat underside of the 1st finger. The bass note for F is the 4th string.

You Needed Me

Words and Music by
Randy Goodrum

Sing:

Option: Capo 2 or 3

I cried a tear, you wiped it dry.
hand when it was cold.

When I was con-fused you cleared my mind.
When I was lost you took me home.

I sold my soul you bought it back for me
You gave me hope when I was at the end,

and held me up and gave me dig-ni-ty.
and turned my lies back in-to truth a-gain.

Some-how you need-ed me. You gave me strength
You ev-en called me friend.

D.S. (Dal Segno) means to go back to the sign 𝄋 until you reach the Fine (end).

119

EASY CHORD TRAX

TEACHER'S AND PLAYER'S NOTE:

This book is a pop, rock chord supplement to the HAL LEONARD GUITAR METHOD or any other beginning guitar method. You can use this book to **strum chords along with exciting pop or rock favorites**. You can strum the chords along with the CD or you can sing the melody and strum the chords (with or without the CD). A Chord Chart is available on page 144. Songs are arranged in the same order that chords are introduced in the HAL LEONARD GUITAR METHOD. Suggested strum numbers are given at the top of each song; you can find the corresponding strums on page 144.

The melodies in this book are not designed to be played by beginners. Players should use the Hal Leonard EASY POP MELODIES supplement for this purpose.

USING THE CD:

Tune your guitar to the tuning notes at the beginning of the CD. The recorded track for each song begins with one full measure (or a partial measure for pick-up notes) of clicks, which sets the tempo of the song. The CD track number is given next to the title of each song. You will probably want to practice the chords on your own before playing along with the CD. The strums on the audio tracks are patterned after the original recordings.

USING THE BOOK:

Tune your guitar following the instructions on page 7. Practice the chords for each song at a steady speed – you may wish to use a metronome or tap your foot. Gradually increase the tempo as you feel comfortable changing chords. You may sing or whistle the melody as you play the chords, or you may have a friend play the melody with you.

ROCK AROUND THE CLOCK

Suggested Strums: 1, 2, 3, 4, 5, 8

By Max C. Freedman and Jimmy DeKnight

Bright Swing Shuffle

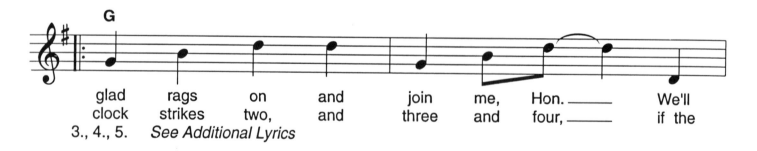

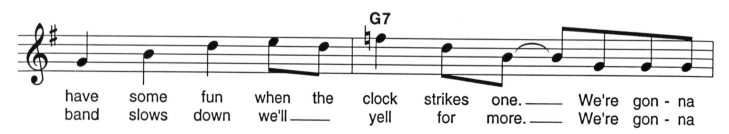

*No chord (Don't play chords until next chord symbol.)

*C

rock   a - round   the   clock   to - night, _____ we're gon - na
rock   a - round   the   clock   to - night, _____ we're gon - na

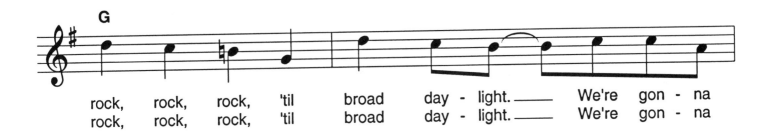

G

rock,   rock,   rock,   'til   broad   day - light. _____ We're gon - na
rock,   rock,   rock,   'til   broad   day - light. _____ We're gon - na

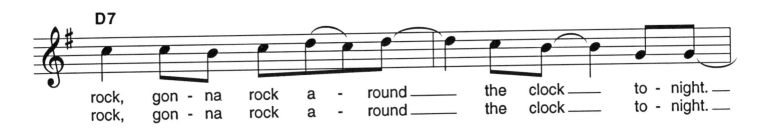

D7

rock,   gon - na   rock   a - round _____ the   clock _____ to - night. __
rock,   gon - na   rock   a - round _____ the   clock _____ to - night. __

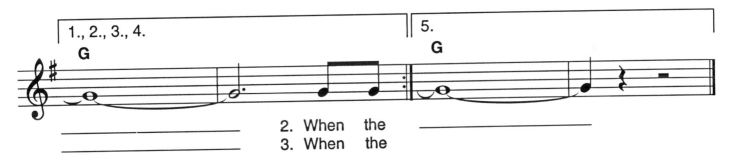

1., 2., 3., 4.

G

5.

G

2. When the
3. When the

*Or play C7

3. When the chimes ring five and six and seven,
   We'll be rockin' up in seventh heav'n,
   We're gonna rock around the clock tonight,
   We're gonna rock, rock, rock, 'til broad daylight
   We're gonna rock, gonna rock around the clock tonight.

4. When it's eight, nine, ten, eleven, too,
   I'll be goin' strong and so will you,
   We're gonna rock around the clock tonight,
   We're gonna rock, rock, rock, 'til broad daylight
   We're gonna rock, gonna rock around the clock tonight.

5. When the clock strikes twelve, we'll cool off, then,
   Start a rockin' 'round the clock again.
   We're gonna rock around the clock tonight,
   We're gonna rock, rock, rock, 'til broad daylight
   We're gonna rock, gonna rock around the clock tonight.

LOVE ME DO ③

Words and Music by
John Lennon and Paul McCartney

Suggested Strums: 3, 4, 5, 6

Moderate Rock

1., 2., 3. Love, love me do, you know I love you.

I'll al - ways be true, so

please, _____ love me

Chorus

do. _____ Whoa, __ love me do. ___

Bridge

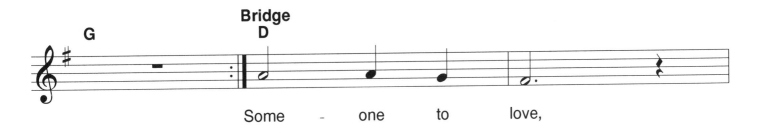

Some - one to love,

some - bod - y new. _____ Some - one to

D.S. al Coda

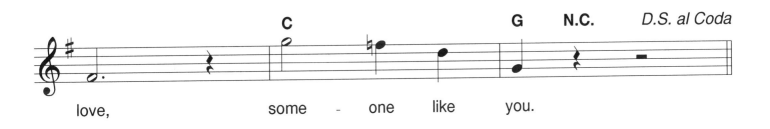

love, some - one like you.

⊕ **Coda**

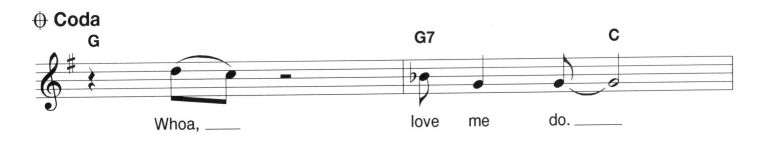

Whoa, ___ love me do. _____

Whoa, ___ love me do. ___

PEGGY SUE ④

Suggested Strums: 1, 2, 8 (double note values)

Words and Music by
Jerry Allison, Norman Petty and Buddy Holly

Bright Rock Beat

Verse

1. If you knew ____ Peg - gy Sue, ____ then you'd
2. Peg - gy Sue, ____ Peg - gy Sue, ____ oh, how

know why I feel blue ____ a - bout Peg - gy, ____
my heart yearns for you, ____ oh, Pa - heg - gy, ____

'bout my Peg - gy Sue. ____
My Pa - hey - gy Sue. ____

Oh, well, I love you, gal, ____ yes, I love you
Oh, well, I love you, gal, ____ yes, I love you

Peg - gy Sue. ____
Peg - gy Sue. ____

Chorus

Peg - gy Sue, ____ Peg - gy Sue, ____

*E♭
pret - ty, pret - ty, pret - ty, pret - ty, Peg - gy Sue. ____ Oh, my

*Move D chord up the neck 1 fret; play strings 3–1.

BIRD DOG ⑤

Suggested Strums: 2, 3, 4, 5, 7, 8

Words and Music by
Boudleaux Bryant

1. John-ny is a jok-er. (He's a bird.) A ver-y fun-ny jok-er.
2. John-ny sings a love song. (Like a bird.) He sings the sweet-est love song.

(He's a bird.) But when he jokes my hon-ey. (He's a dog.) His
(You ever heard.) But when he sings to my gal. (What a howl.) To

jok-in' ain't so fun-ny. (What a dog.) John-ny is the jok-er that's a
me he's just a wolf dog. (On the prowl.) John-ny wants to fly a-way and

try-in to steal my ba-by. (He's a bird dog.)
pup-py love my ba-by. (He's a bird dog.)

Chorus

Hey, bird dog, get a-way from my quail. — Hey, bird dog, you're on —

— the wrong trail. Bird dog, you'd bet-ter leave my lov-ey dove a-lone. —

* Optional.
**You may wish to play C7 on the C chords.

Hey, bird dog, get a-way from my chick. __

Hey, bird dog, you'd bet-ter get a-way quick. __ Bird dog, you'd bet-ter find a

chick-en lit-tle of your own. __

Verse

3. John-ny kissed the teach-er. (He's a bird.) He tip-toed up to reach her.

(He's a bird.) Well, he's the teach-er's pet now. (He's a dog.) What

he wants he can get now. (What a dog.) He ev-en made the teach-er let him

sit next to my ba-by. (He's a bird dog.)

Coda

chick-en lit-tle of your own. __

CANDLE IN THE WIND ⑥

Words and Music by
Elton John and Bernie Taupin

Suggested Strums: 1, 2, 3, 6, 8

Moderate Ballad
Verse

130

made   you change __   your name. ___
Mar - i - lyn   was found   in the nude. ___

Chorus

seems   to   me __   you   lived your   life __   like   a   can - dle   in ___   the   wind. __

___   Nev - er   know - ing   who __   to   cling   to   when the

rain   set   in. __   And   I   would have   liked __   to   have

known   you, _____   but   I   was   just   a   kid. __   Your

can - dle   burned   out   long _____   be - fore _____   your

leg - end   ev - er   did. _____

LONG TALL SALLY ⑦

Suggested Strums: 1, 2, 3, 4, 5, 6, 8

Words and Music by Enotris Johnson,
Richard Penniman and Robert Blackwell

Bright Boogie Shuffle

*Or play C7

ELEANOR RIGBY ⑧

Suggested Strums: 2, 3, 4, 5, 6, 7, 8

Words and Music by
John Lennon and Paul McCartney

Moderately

Ah _____ look at all ____ the lone - ly peo - ple!

1. E - lea - nor Rig - by, picks up the rice ___ in the church ⌣ where a wed - ding has been,
2. Fath - er Mc - Ken - zie, writ - ing the words of a ser - mon that no ___ one will hear, ___
3. E - lea - nor Rig - by, died in the church and was bur - ied a - long ___ with her name,

___ lives in a dream. _____ Waits at the win - dow,
___ no one comes near. _____ Look at him work - ing,
___ no - bod - y came. _____ Fath - er Mc - Ken - zie,

wear - ing the face ____ that she keeps ____ in a jar ___ by the door, ___
darn - ing his socks ___ in the night ___ when there's no - bod - y there, ___
wip - ing the dirt ___ from his hands ___ as he walks ___ from the grave, ___

who is it for? _____ ⎫
what does he care? _____ ⎬ All the lone - ly peo - ple, where
no one was saved. _____ ⎭

do they all ___ come from? _____ All the lone - ly peo -

play 3 times (3rd time,
D.C. al Fine)

- ple, where do they all ___ be - long? _____

133

TAKIN' CARE OF BUSINESS

Suggested Strums: 3, 4, 5

Words and Music by
Randy Bachman

Moderate Rock

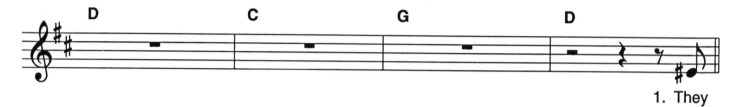

1. They

Verse

get up ev - 'ry morn - in' from the 'larm clock's warn - in', take the
eas - y as __ fish - in', you could be a mu - si - cian if

eight fif - teen in - to the ci - ty. There's a whis - tle up a - bove and peo - ple
you can make sounds loud or mel- low. Get a sec- ond hand gui- tar, chan - ces

push- in' peo - ple shov- in' and the girls who try to look pret - ty. And if your
are you'll go far if you get in with the right bunch of fel- lows. Peo - ple

train's on time you can get to work by nine and start your slav- in' job to get your
see you havin' fun just a - ly- in' in the sun. __ Tell them that you like it this way.

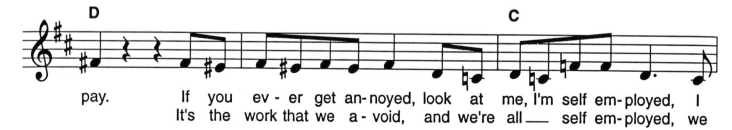

pay. If you ev - er get an-noyed, look at me, I'm self em-ployed, I
It's the work that we a - void, and we're all __ self em-ployed, we

SURFIN' U.S.A. ⑩

Suggested Strums: 3, 4, 5, 7, 8

Music by Chuck Berry
Lyric by Brian Wilson

Bright Rock

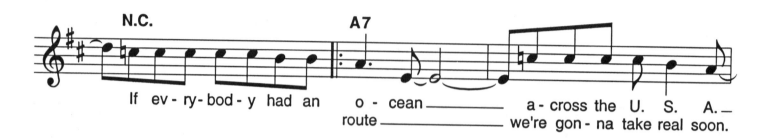

If ev - ry - bod - y had an o - cean _____ a - cross the U. S. A. _____
route _____ we're gon - na take real soon.

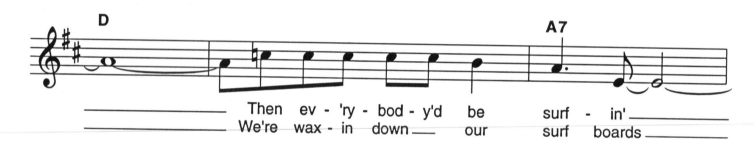

_____ Then ev - 'ry - bod - y'd be surf - in' _____
_____ We're wax - in down _____ our surf boards _____

— like Cal - i - for - ni - a. _____ You'd see them wear - in' their
— we can't _____ wait for June. _____ We'll all be gone for the

bag - gies, _____ huar - a - chi san - dals too. _____
sum - mer, _____ we're on sa - fa - ri to stay. _____

— A bush - y bush - y blonde hair - do, _____ surf - in' U. S. A. _____
_____ Tell the teach - er we're surf - in', _____ surf - in' U. S. A. _____

You'll catch 'em surf - in' at Del Mar, _____
At Hag - gar - ty's _____ and Swam - i's _____

___ Ven - tu - ra Coun - try Line. _____ San - ta Cruz and
___ Pac - if - ic Pal - i - sades. _____ San O - nofre and

Tress - els, _____ Aus - tra - lia's Nar - a - bine. _____
Sun - set, _____ Re - don - do Beach, L. A. _____

___ All o - ver Man - hat - tan _____ and down Do - he - ny way. __
___ All o - ver La Jol - la, _____ at Wai - a - me - a Bay. __

_____ Ev - 'ry - bod - y's gone surf - in, _____ surf - in' U. S. A. __
_____ Ev - 'ry - bod - y's gone surf - in', _____ surf-in' U. S. A. __

_____ We'll all be plan - nin' out a ___

BLUE SUEDE SHOES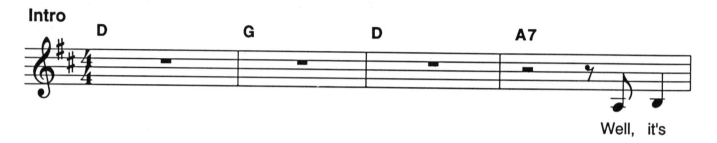

Suggested Strums: 1, 2, 3, 4, 5, 8

Words and Music by
Carl Lee Perkins

Bright Boogie

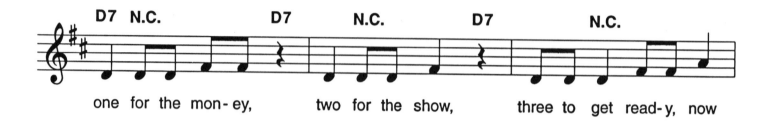

Well, it's

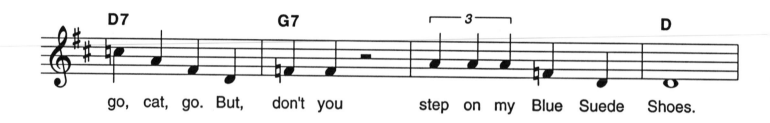

one for the mon- ey, two for the show, three to get read-y, now

go, cat, go. But, don't you step on my Blue Suede Shoes.

You can do an-y-thing,— but lay off of my Blue Suede Shoes. —

1. Well, you can knock me down, — step on my face, —
burn my house, — steal — my car, —

N.C.   D7   N.C.

slan-der my name all o - ver the place. Do an-y-thing that you
drink my cider from my old fruit jar.

D7   N.C.   D7

want to do, bu uh - uh, hon-ey, lay off of my shoes.

G7   3   D

Don't you step on my Blue Suede Shoes. You can

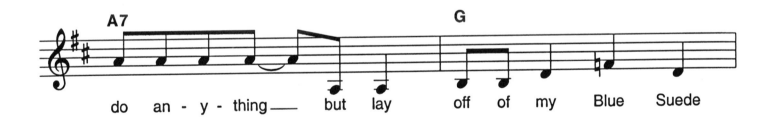

A7   G

do an - y - thing but lay off of my Blue Suede

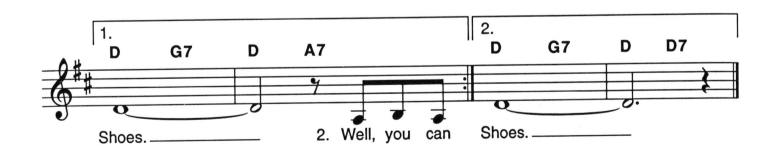

1.
D   G7   D   A7   2.   D   G7   D   D7

Shoes. 2. Well, you can Shoes.

AFRICA UNITE

Suggested Strums: 3, 4, 5, 6

Words and Music by
Bob Marley

Moderate Reggae

*or play C7.

DUKE OF EARL ⑬

Suggested Strums: 2, 3, 4, 6, 10

Words and Music by Earl Edwards,
Eugene Dixon and Bernice Williams

Moderate Rock

As —

I _____ walk through this world, no - thing can stop the
When _____ I hold _____ you, you _____ will be the

Duke of Earl. _____ And you _____ are my girl, _____ and
Duchess of Earl. When I walk _____ through my Duke - dom, the

no one can hurt you. Yes, I'm _____ gon - na
par - a - dise we will share. I'm _____ gon - na

love you _____ let me hold you, _____ 'cause I'm the Duke of
love you _____ let me hold you, _____ 'cause I'm the Duke of

1. Earl. _____

2. Earl. _____

142

STRUMS

The strum symbols and their meanings are as follows:

⊓ — Down stroke
V — Up stroke
X — Dampening with the hand

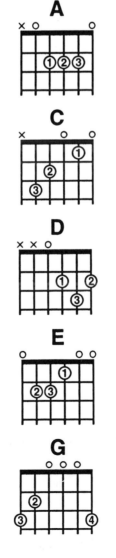

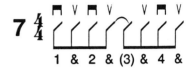

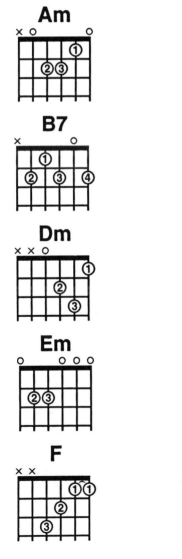

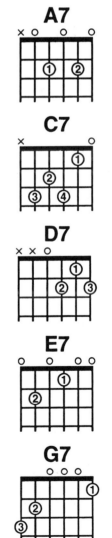

Eighth notes in the above strums may be played even or uneven (dotted) depending on the style of the music.

CHORD CHART

In this chart you will find the chords learned in this book as well as several other common chords you may see in music you are playing.

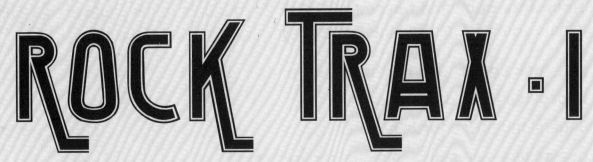

ROCK TRAX · 1

How to Improvise Rock for Beginners

USING THE BOOK:

Tune your guitar following the instructions on page 7.

Use *Rock Trax-1* to get started with creating your own music. *Rock Trax-1* begins at an easy level with no-fault improvisation – you can't play a wrong note. It then progresses into a 12-bar blues which will lead you right into rock leads and power chords.

Practice playing the "Rock Strum" for each Trax and record it if you have a tape recorder; then practice the lead guitar "Solo Licks" and scales that will help you put together your own solos. You may play solos along with the taped "Rock Strum" or with another player. If two guitars play together, alternating rhythm and lead guitar roles is a fun challenge.

As you learn how melodies and chords combine, try making up your own songs or instrumental solos. You can either tape record them, write them down on paper, or sequence them on a MIDI compatible computer.

How To Use Rock Trax

This **Rock Trax Book and Cassette/CD Pak** is your door to the world of rock guitar. By the time you finish playing this material, you will be able to:

- play **rock chords** and **rhythm guitar** parts
- **improvise lead rock solos**
- understand how **chords** are built
- **use scales** as resource material for lead solos
- locate rock finger **patterns on the fretboard**

Rock Trax is a *no-fault* approach to learning how to improvise. It is designed as a step-by-step method which takes the fear out of playing your own rock solos. This is accomplished by beginning with a limited number of notes which are played over a simple rock background. Gradually you will add more notes, chords and rock licks until you are covering the entire fretboard. The **Rock Trax Cassette/CD** lets you practice in the privacy of your room.

To get the most out of the **Rock Trax Book:**

- Play each of the new **Rhythm Guitar Chords** using the rock strum.
- Play the **Lead Guitar** finger patterns up and down until your fingers are well acquainted with them.
- Listen to each **Solo Lick** on the cassette/CD; then practice it until your fingers can play in with ease.

The Rock Trax Cassette/CD gives you a great rock band to back-up your Rhythm Guitar part or Lead Guitar solo. Each of the Rock Trax cuts is deliberately long enough so you can try out many solo improvisation ideas without having to rewind the cassette or reset your CD player as often. In addition to the Rock Trax #1 through #8, the **cassette/CD demonstrates each Solo Lick and new techniques such as slides, bends, hammer-ons and pull-offs.**

Although rock is normally played on an electric guitar, you can learn almost as much by practicing the patterns on an acoustic guitar. If you have an electric guitar, experiment with the tone settings, but don't use them as a substitute for accuracy and careful listening.

So, welcome to the world of **Rock Trax.**

Rock Trax #1: Rhythm Guitar

You can play rhythm guitar (back-up) with the band on the cassette by using any one of the three chords on this page. Practice each chord with the strumming patterns indicated; then try them with the **Rock Trax** cassette/CD.

The Em Chord

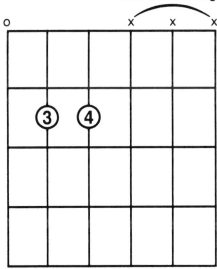

The E Chord

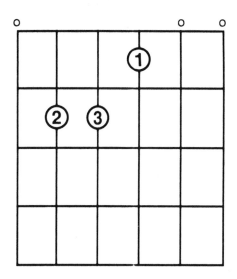

The E Power Chord (also sometimes called E(no 3rd))

Mute with 1st finger.

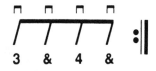

The E power chord is fingered differently from the Em chord because it is moved up and down the neck as a bar chord (You will learn more about that when you play Rock Trax #2). Notice that **only strings 6 through 4 are sounded.** The x over strings 1, 2 and 3 reminds you not to strum these strings. Mute strings 3-1 with your first finger.

Rock Strum (Play all down strokes ⊓.)

Repeat many times using each Chord form as you play along with **Rock Trax #1.**

Rock Trax #1: Lead Guitar

Your first lead guitar solo improvisation is based on only four notes. This is done so you can concentrate on making the most of a small amount of material. Many of the greatest rock stars often take three or four notes and play around with them rhythmically in their solo breaks. Below you will find these four notes (E G B and D) in two different places on the fretboard. Watch the fingerings carefully as you practice each.

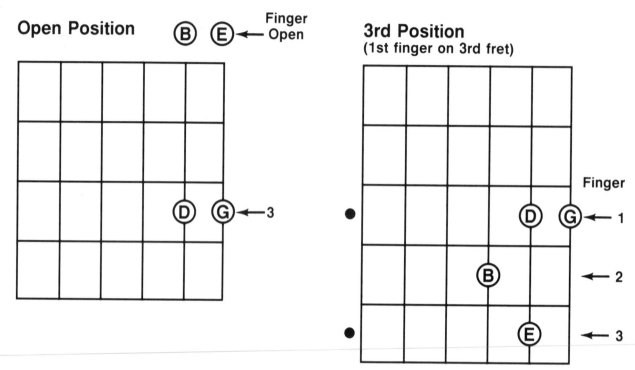

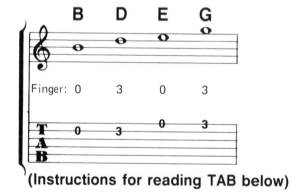

(Instructions for reading TAB below)

Reading Music and Tablature

Lead patterns in this book are written in both notes and tablature (TAB). Below is a guide to reading tablature:

Guitar tablature (TAB) is a means of notating finger positions by giving the number of the fret where the finger belongs. The numbers are placed on the line which corresponds to a string on the guitar. If there is an "o", play that string open.

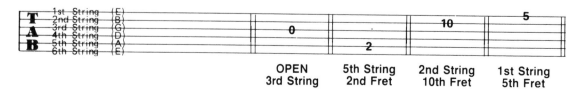

Rock Trax #1: Solo Licks

Most lead rock guitar players string together a series of **licks** (short motives or finger patterns) to make their solos. Below are only a few of the licks that are possible using the notes E G B and D. Practice the licks until your fingers know them well; then change the rhythms and note patterns to make your own licks. Each lick is demonstrated on the **Rock Trax** cassette/CD. The TAB gives you the 3rd position indications; practice each lick also in open position.

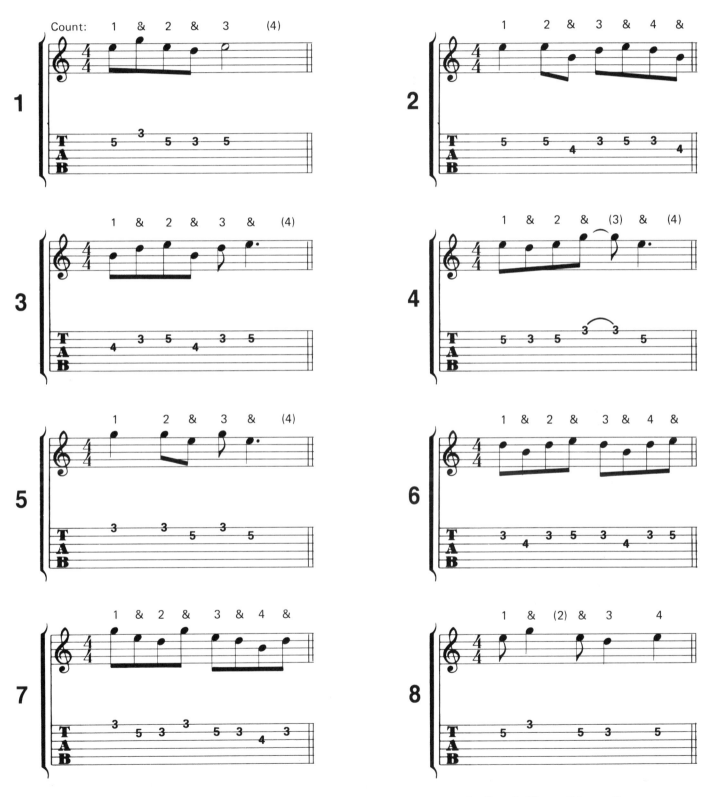

Now play these licks and those you have made up with **Rock Trax #1** on the cassette/CD. Don't be afraid to repeat a good idea. Squeeze a lot of music out of these four notes by playing interesting rhythms.

Rock Trax #2: Rhythm Guitar

The rhythm guitar part for **Rock Trax** #2 uses the E chords you already know and the new A chords below. Study each form and practice the strumming patterns.

The **Am** Chord

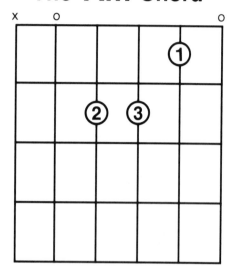

The **A** Chord

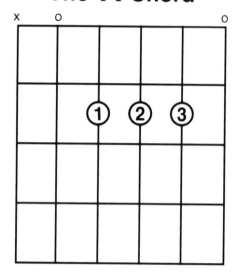

The **A7** Chord

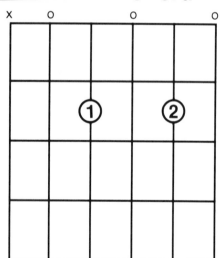

The **A** Power Chord

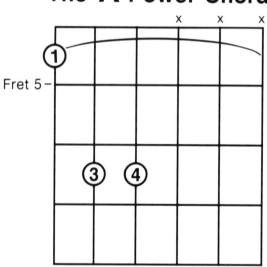

Rock Strum (Play with Rock Trax #2)

E* (4 times)   A* (4 times)

4/4

| 1 (&) 2 & 3 & 4 & | 1 (&) 2 & 3 & 4 & |

*Use any form of the E or A chords studied.

Rock Trax #2: Lead Guitar

The E Minor Pentatonic (Blues/Rock) Scale

The most common scale used in rock is the **pentatonic** (5-toned). This scale can be played by adding the note A to the notes used in Rock Trax #1. The pentatonic scale based on E is spelled **E G A B D,** and you will find a full 6-string version of it below. The theory behind this scale will be explained more fully later.

Open Position

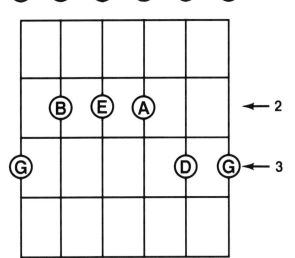

Notice the fingering pattern above.

Extended position

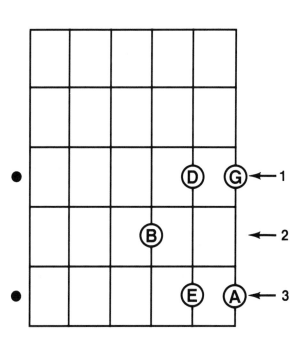

Open Position Notes

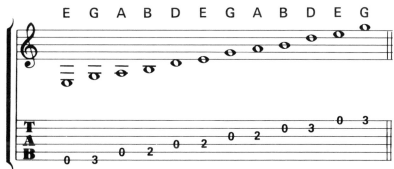

Extended Position Notes

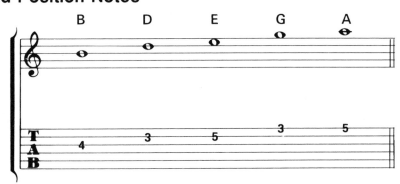

The Slide

The **slide** is one of the left-hand techniques that gives rock its characteristic sound. The slide is played in the following manner:

- Place your left-hand third finger on second string D (3rd fret).

- Pluck the note D and maintain pressure on the string as you slide to the 5th fret.

The most effective slide possibilities are those given below:

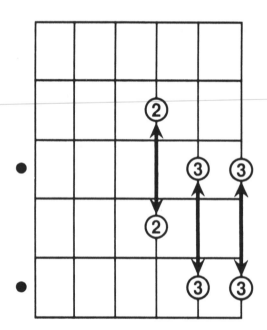

Slides can be used in a number of different ways. Practice each example below; then listen to them on the **Rock Trax Cassette/CD.**

Rock Trax #2: Solo Licks

Below are some more licks that can be played with **Rock Trax #2.** Add these to those you learned already, and you should have the material for an interesting lead rock solo. The symbol > is called an **accent**, and it tells you to play that note with more force. The chord letters which appear over each lick below tell you whether to play the lick over an E or an A measure. Notice that the note E is the most important note in the E licks and the A is the most important note in the A measures.

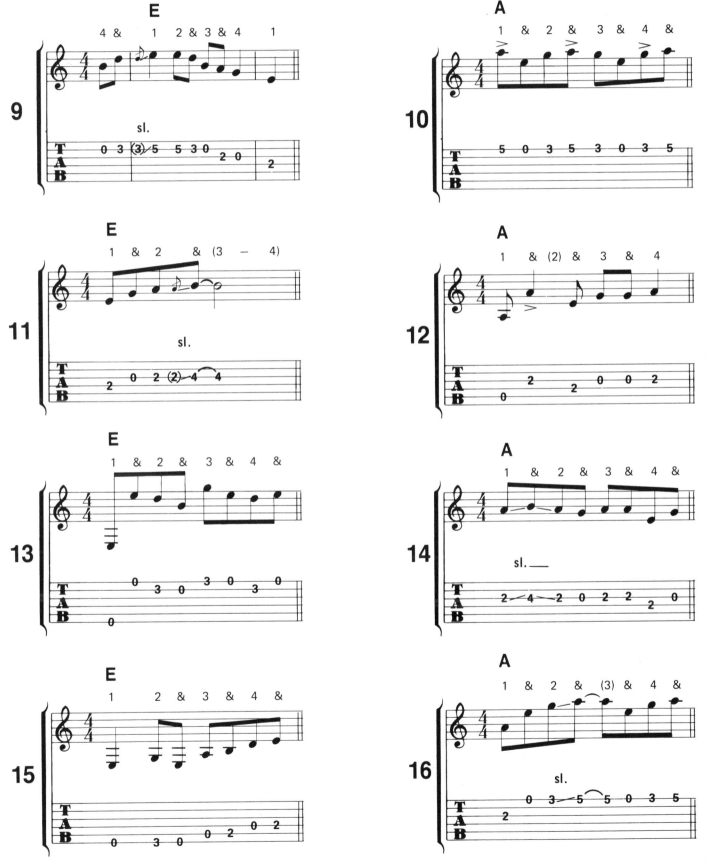

Bending Notes

Bending, like sliding, is another of the left-hand techniques commonly used in rock. The bend is played in the following manner:

- Place your third finger on the third string at the 7th fret.

- Pluck the string; then push the string upward with your third finger while maintaining pressure.

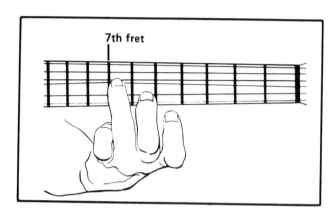

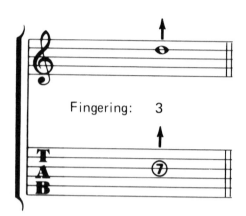

You will find that lighter gauge strings make bending easier. The bend illustrated at the 7th fret can be played in three basic ways:

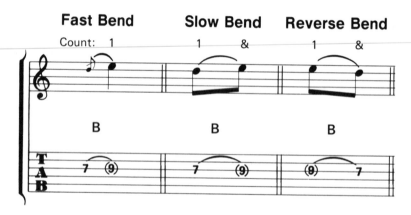

In addition to bending the string upwards, you can bend by pulling the string toward your palm. Try this with your first and third fingers.

Play these two examples of bending on the E pentatonic; then listen to them on the cassette/CD.

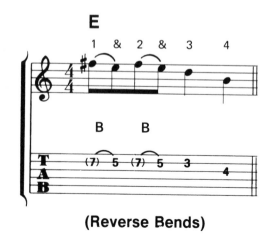

(Reverse Bends)

(Slow Bend)

154

Major Scales and Major Chords

A **half step** is the smallest interval on the guitar—the distance from one fret to the next.

A **whole step** is the interval between one note and another two frets higher or lower. One whole step equals two half steps.

A **major scale** is a series of eight notes arranged in a pattern of whole and half steps as follows:

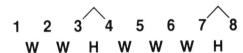

Now pick up your guitar and play the major scale on the first string as illustrated to the right. As you play, memorize the pattern of whole and half steps by saying it out loud (whole, whole, half,. . .). Try the major scale on each string—the pattern is the same. You may have learned this pattern in school as *Do Re Mi Fa Sol La Ti Do*. Play the scales both up and down the string.

A **chord** is the simultaneous sounding of three or more notes. A **major chord** consists of notes **1,3,and 5** of any major scale played at the same time. Play notes **1**(open) **3** (fret 4) and **5** (fret 7) on the **third string—G Major Scale.**

When these notes are played together they form the **G Major Chord** (written **G**). The chord tones are named the **root** (1), **third** (3) and **fifth** (5), and the chord is named after the root.

The Major Chord

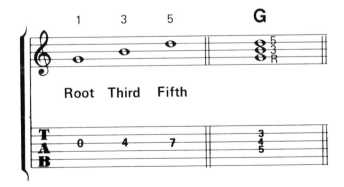

Minor Scales and Minor Chords

Minor Scale   **E Minor Pentatonic**

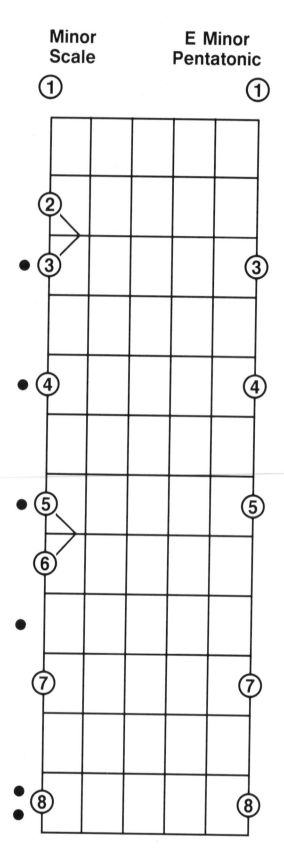

A **minor scale** is also a series of eight notes arranged in a pattern of whole and half steps as follows:

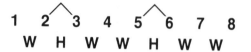

Notice that the half steps come between tones **2 to 3** and between **5 to 6.** Contrast this pattern with the major scale where the half steps occur between **3 to 4** and **7 to 8.**

Now play the minor scale on the sixth string and compare it to the major scale on page 12.

Three symbols are used in music to change the way a note is played:

A **flat** ♭ lowers a note by a half step (1 fret).

A **sharp** ♯ raises a note by a half step (1 fret).

A **natural** ♮ cancels a sharp or a flat.

Flats, sharps and naturals are always written to the left of a note ♭♩ and to the right of a letter name **F♯**.

Another way to think of a minor scale is the way jazz guitarists do—as a major scale with alterations:

Minor Scale = Altered Major Scale

1   2   (♭3)   4   5   (♭6)   (♭7)   8

The **minor pentatonic** uses tones 1   3   4   5 and 7 of the minor scale. Play the E minor pentatonic you already know on string 1.

The **minor chord** uses tones **1**   **3**   and **5** of the minor scale. Compare with the major chord (jazz players think of minor as **1**   ♭**3**   **5** — an altered major chord).

The Minor Chord   Gm

Root   Third   Fifth

Rock Trax #3: Rhythm Guitar

The 12-Bar Blues/Rock

Rock and Roll was born in the 50's as a new form of black 12-bar blues. Even today, most rock and jazz players start out by learning the 12-bar (12-measure) blues/rock form. The 12-bar form in the key of E uses several new chords given below. Practice each of them; then play the rock strum with the cassette/CD.

The E7 Chord
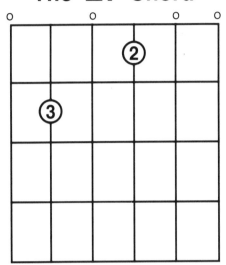

The A7 Bar Chord
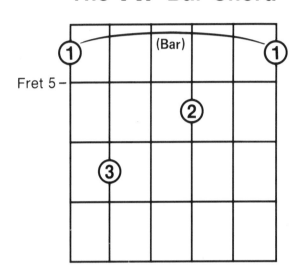

The B7 Bar Chord
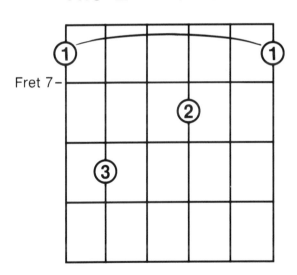

The B Power Chord
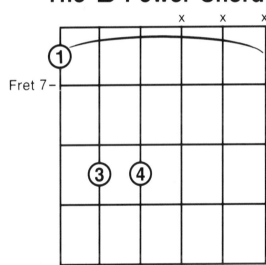

Rock Strum (Substitute the E, A, and B power chords if you wish.)

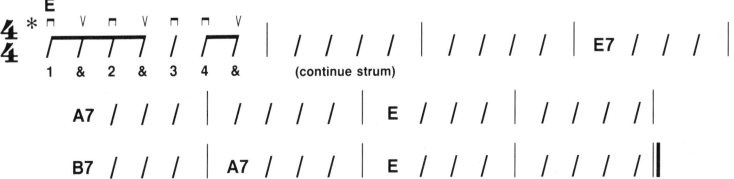

*or play all down strokes (⊓)

Rock Trax #3: Lead Guitar and Solo Licks

The lead guitar patterns for Rock Trax #3 are based on the E minor pentatonic that you have been playing. If you wish you could add the 7th fret note **B** on the first string. Practice the solo licks below with the cassette. Notice which licks go with which chords. The first time through the tape, you may wish to play only the roots of the chords with each measure. This will ensure that you are hearing which chord is being played.

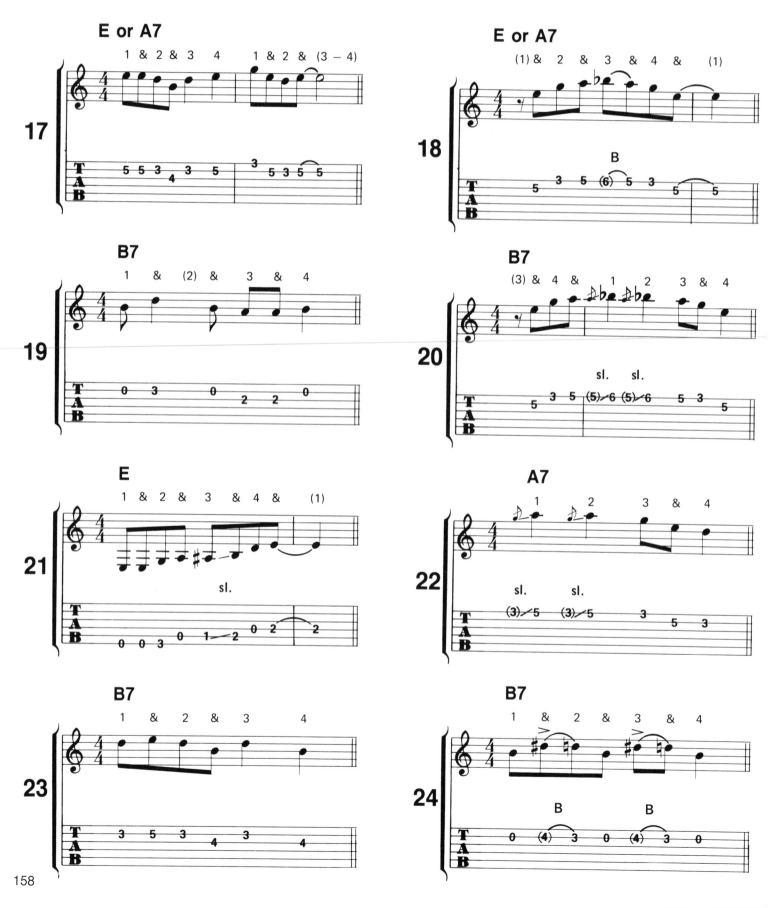

Rock Trax #4: Rhythm Guitar

Rock Trax #4 uses the 12-bar blues/rock form in the new key of A. Below are the new chords you will need to know:

The **A** Bar Chord

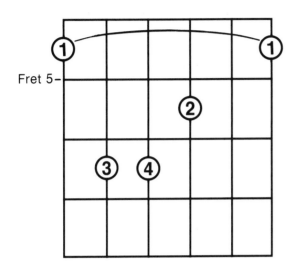

The **D7** Bar Chord

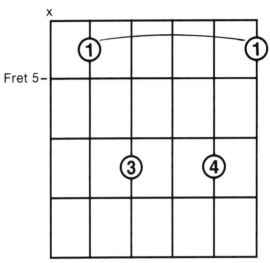

To play the E7 Bar Chord, move the D7 Bar Chord to Fret 7.

The **E7** Chord (4-string)

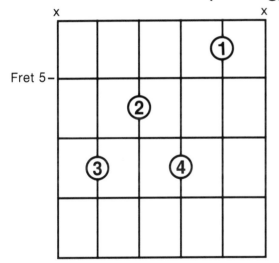

To play D7, move E7 to Fret 3.

The **D** Power Chord

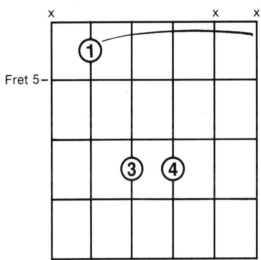

To play the E Power Chord, move the D Power Chord to Fret 7.

Use open-position chords, bar chords or power chords for the 12-bar blues/rock pattern below. How many versions of these chords can you play with **Rock Trax #4?**

Rock Strum:

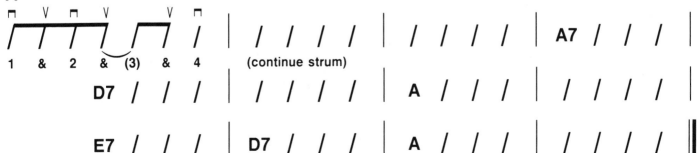

*or play all down strokes (⊓)

159

Rock Trax #4: Lead Guitar

The A minor Pentatonic

Before you look at the fretboard below, see if you can construct an A minor scale on the fifth string A; then play the pentatonic tones 1 3 4 5 and 7. Below are two positions for playing the A minor pentatonic — one in open position and one at the 5th position (1st finger at the 5th fret).

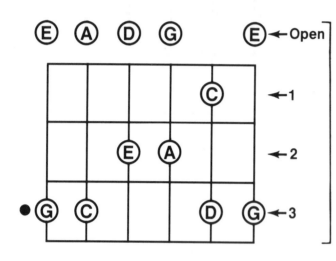

Open Position

As you play through the open-position notes, you will see that the only difference between this and the E minor pentatonic is that the note **C** replaces the note **B**.

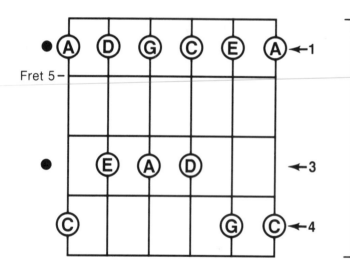

5th Position

This finger pattern is derived from the E minor pentatonic pattern in open position. Since there are no open strings at the 5th position, the fingering has to change.

Memorize the finger pattern:

1	1	1	1	1	1
	3	3	3		
4				4	4

Open Position

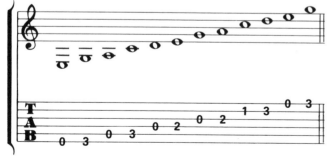

5th Position

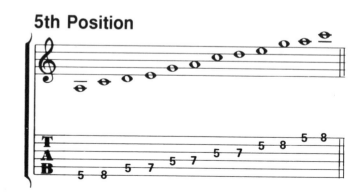

160

Rock Trax #4: Solo Licks

Most of the solo licks for Rock Trax #4 are given in the 5th position, but you should experiment with playing similar ideas in open position.

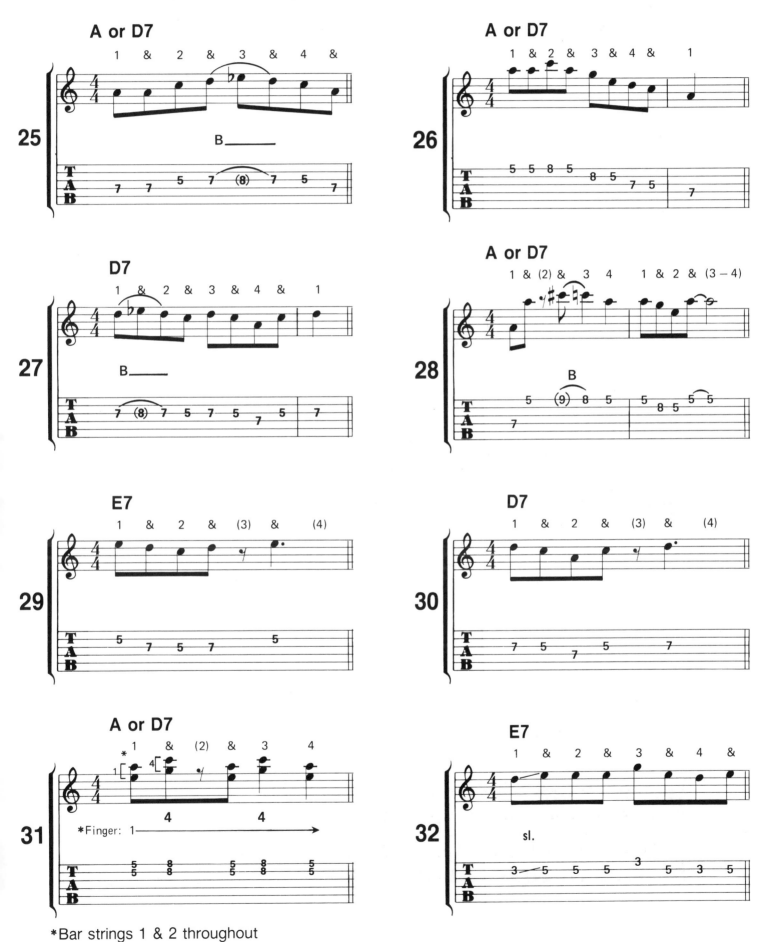

*Bar strings 1 & 2 throughout
with 1st finger.

The Complete Fretboard (Frets 1-15)

You already have gained a considerable knowledge of the fretboard. To become a masterful rock guitarist, you must continue to develop this knowledge. Some important uses for fretboard understanding are:

- **where to play bar chords and power chords**

- **the development of scales**

- **alternate fingers**

To the right is a fretboard which already has some letter names written on it. It is up to you to finish writing in the rest of the letter names. Here are a few handy tips to guide you:

1. Finish writing in all of the regular letter names. These notes are all part of the C major scale. Remember:

> **Half Steps: E → F and B → C**

2. Before you go on, memorize the names of the notes on strings 6 and 5 — they tell you where to place your 1st bar finger for all bar chords and power chords. Notice that most of the important chord names occur where there is a fret dot.

3. The empty frets you left between F→G, G→A, A→B, C→D and D→E can now be filled in with sharps and flats. Each of these frets can be called by two names. See string 1, fret 2. The rule for when to use which is:

> **Ascending notes use sharps ♯**
>
> **Descending notes use flats ♭**

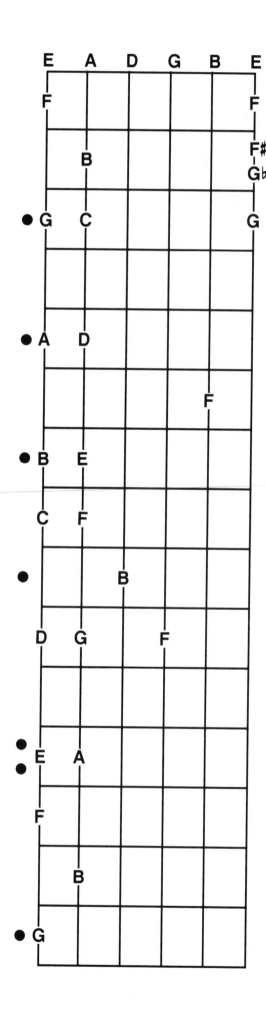

Rock Trax #5: Rhythm Guitar

Rock Trax #5 is a typical section of a rock piece where the band plays a sequence of two or three chords over which the lead guitar player improvises. Play the new chords below or any other forms of **Am** and **G** that you already know with the cassette.

The **Am** Bar Chord

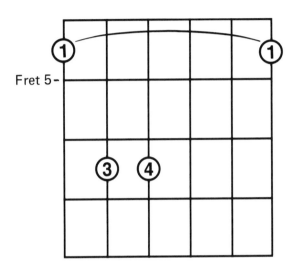

The **G** Chord

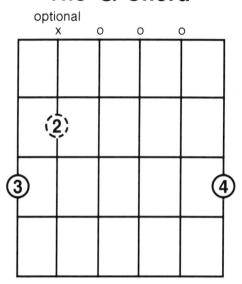

The **G** Bar Chord

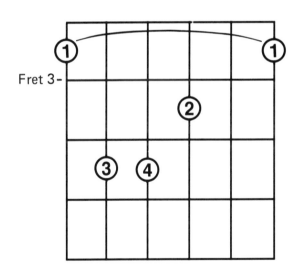

The **G** Power Chord

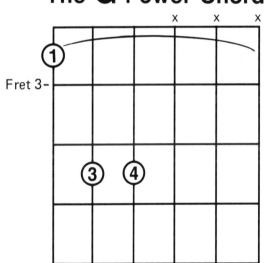

Rock Strum:

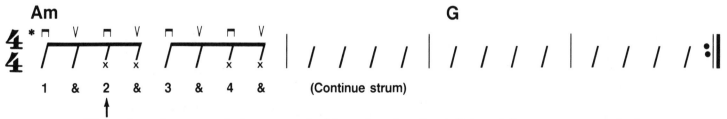

(Continue strum)

The x is a dampened strum created by releasing the left-hand finger pressure, but still touching the strings.

*or play all down strokes (⊓)

Rock Trax #5: Lead Guitar

The Major Pentatonic:

The Major Pentatonic scale is derived from the major scale in much the same way that the minor pentatonic scale was. Before reading on to the explanation below, play a major scale on your third string G.

The Major Penatonic uses notes 1 2 3 5 and 6 of the major scale. Below is the G major scale, its major pentatonic and the G chord.

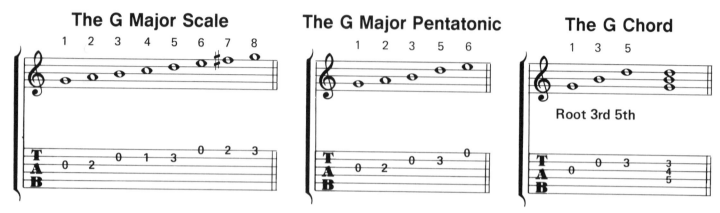

Review the notes in the A minor scale, pentatonic and Am chord you already know.

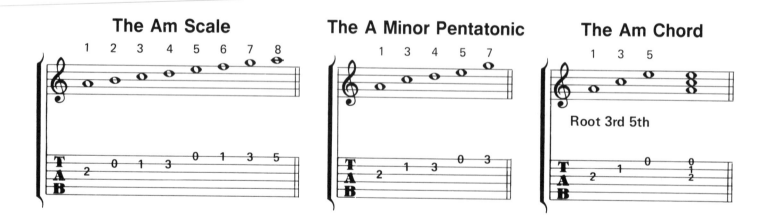

Improvising over chords

When you improvise over a major or minor chord, follow these guidelines:

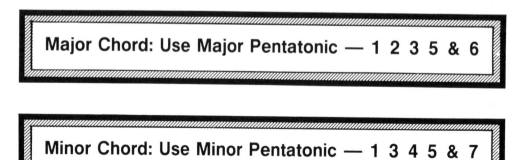

Major Chord: Use Major Pentatonic — 1 2 3 5 & 6

Minor Chord: Use Minor Pentatonic — 1 3 4 5 & 7

The Hammer-on and Pull-off

The Hammer-on (Slur)

Another typical rock technique, the **hammer-on**, is named for the action of the left-hand fingers on the fretboard. The musical name for the hammer-on is the **slur**, which consists of **two different pitches connected by a curved line**. Don't confuse the hammer-on or slur with the **tie**—two notes on the same pitch connected by a curved line. Play the hammer-on as follows:

- **With your left-hand, first finger down (or with an open string — as in the second example), pick the first note below;**

- **Then hammer your third finger down on the string to sound the second note.**

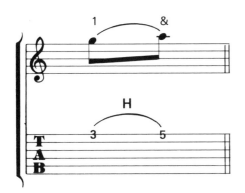 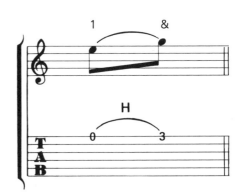

The Pull-off (Slur)

The **pull-off** is the physical opposite of the hammer-on and is also a slur. Play the pull-off as follows:

- **Starting with both left-hand fingers on the string (or one if the second note is open), pick the first note;**

- **Then maintain finger pressure as you pull your third finger toward the palm of your hand. This will sound the second of the two notes.**

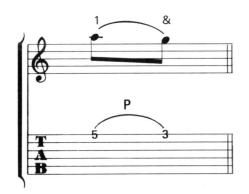 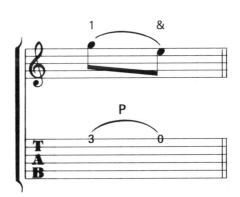

You will find these Hammer-ons and Pull-offs demonstrated on the cassette/CD.

Rock Trax #5: Solo Licks

The eight solo licks on this page all work off of the A minor or G major pentatonic notes from page 164. They also make use of the hammer-on and pull-off you just learned. When you have practiced these licks with **Rock Trax #5**, work out some licks of your own.

Improvisation Tip: Rests are the windows of music — Let some light shine in by leaving some open spaces.

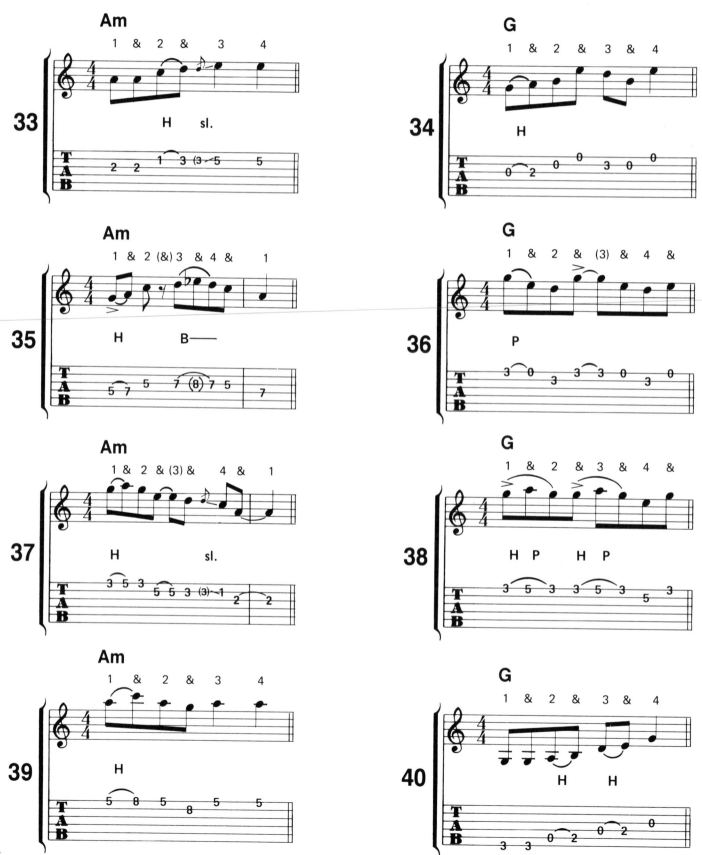

Rock Trax #6: Rhythm Guitar

Rock Trax #6 uses a **G** and an **Em** chord to achieve a mellow or ballad-like quality. These chords sound a bit more contemporary when they are played with an **added 9th above the root** — written **G(add9)**

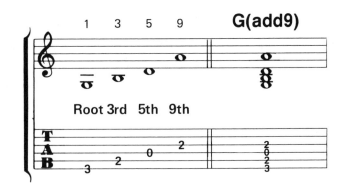

Below are two new **add9** chords which can be played with **Rock Trax #6**.

The G (add9) Chord
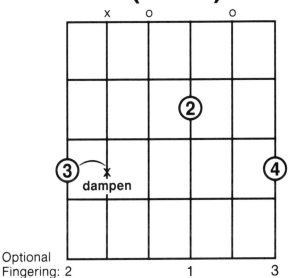

Optional Fingering: 2   1   3

The Em (add9) Chord
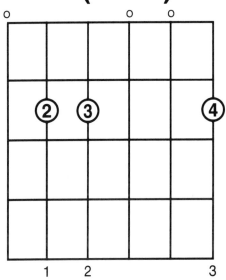

You should feel free to substitute any other form of **G** or **Em** for the rhythm guitar part on **Rock Trax #6**.

Chord Tip: If you don't know how to play a chord with <u>numbers</u> after the letters, substitute the simpler form of the chord you know. Examples: G7→ G or Am7→ Am.

Rock Strum:

Rock Trax #6: Lead Guitar

Relative Majors and Minors

The two lead guitar scale patterns you need for **Rock Trax #6** are the **G major scale/pentatonic** and the **E minor scale/pentatonic** — already familiar territory. There is, however, a unique relationship between these two scales which you should know about — **they share the same notes.**

- **The E minor scale is the <u>relative minor</u> of the G major scale.**

- **The G major scale is the <u>relative major</u> of the E minor scale.**

Here is the nature of the relationship:

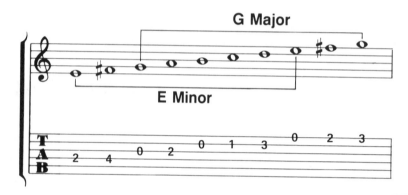

Scale Tip: The relative minor scale starts 3 frets lower than its relative major. They both have the same key signature. (Play the E minor (frets: 0 → 12) and the G major (frets: 3 → 15) scales on the first string.)

On the fretboard to the right you will find the notes for both E minor and G major in an extended location at the 7th fret. Since the pentatonic notes are the most important, you will see that they are circled, while the remaining notes are given as plain letters.

Improvisation Tip: The <u>root</u> (letter name) of a chord is like home base — **start your leads by "hanging around home."**

Check your understanding: What is the relative minor scale for C major?

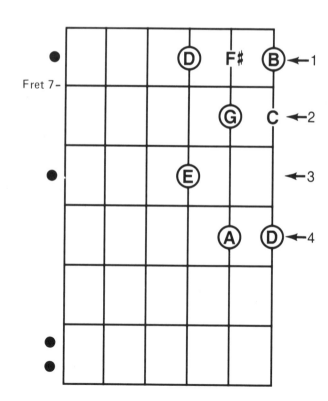

(ʌ :ɹǝʍsu∀)

Rock Trax #6: Solo Licks

Since both the **G** and the **Em** chords use the same notes for improvising, you should pay particular attention to the **root** of each chord. Use the G or the E as "home base" from which you play off of the G or Em chord tones. Here are some solo licks to start you off; then make up your own.

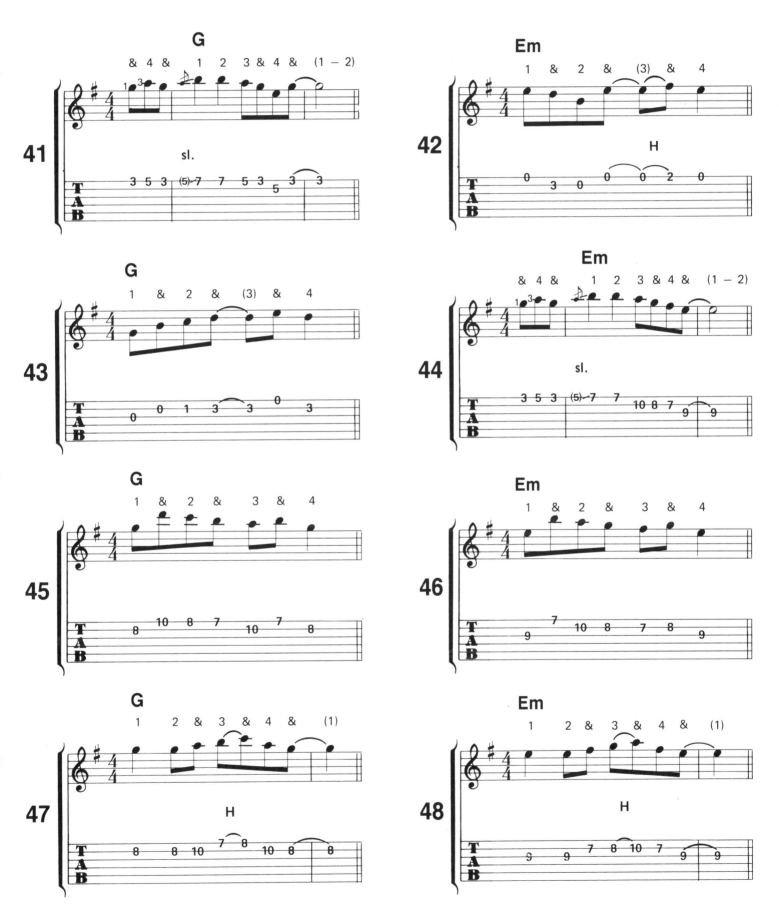

Rock Trax #7: Rhythm Guitar

One of the most common rock chord progressions — two major chords a whole step apart — serves as the basis for **Rock Trax #7**. The chords you will need to know are **D** and **C**. Substitutions for these straight major chords can include **D(add9)** and **C(add9)** given below or the **D and C Power Chords**. (See page 159 for the D Power Chord; move it to the 3rd fret for the C Power Chord.)

The D Major Chord

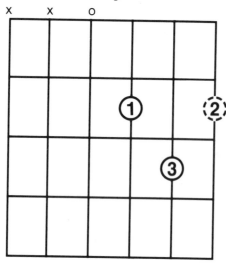

To play **D(add9)** subtract the 2nd finger on string 1.

The C Major Chord

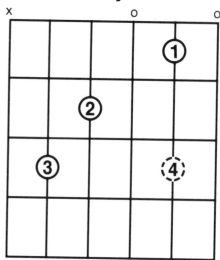

To play **C(add9)** add the 4th finger on the 2nd string, Fret 3.

The chord pattern for **Rock Trax #7** is a good one for trying strum variations. Below are two different ways to play the rhythm guitar part with the cassette/CD.

Rock Strum:

or

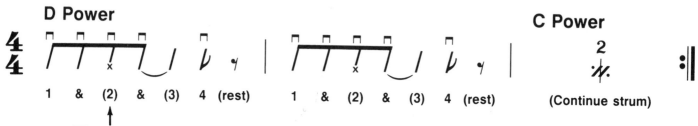

The x on beat 2 is a dampened strum created by releasing the left-hand finger pressure, but still touching the strings.

Rock Trax #7: Lead Guitar

The **C and D** major scales, their pentatonics and chords are given below as source material for your solo lead guitar improvisations. On the fretboard below, pentatonic notes (1 2 3 5 & 6) are circled, and notes 4 and 7 are not.

Fretboard Tip: Any finger pattern or chord on C can be moved up the neck two frets to become D.

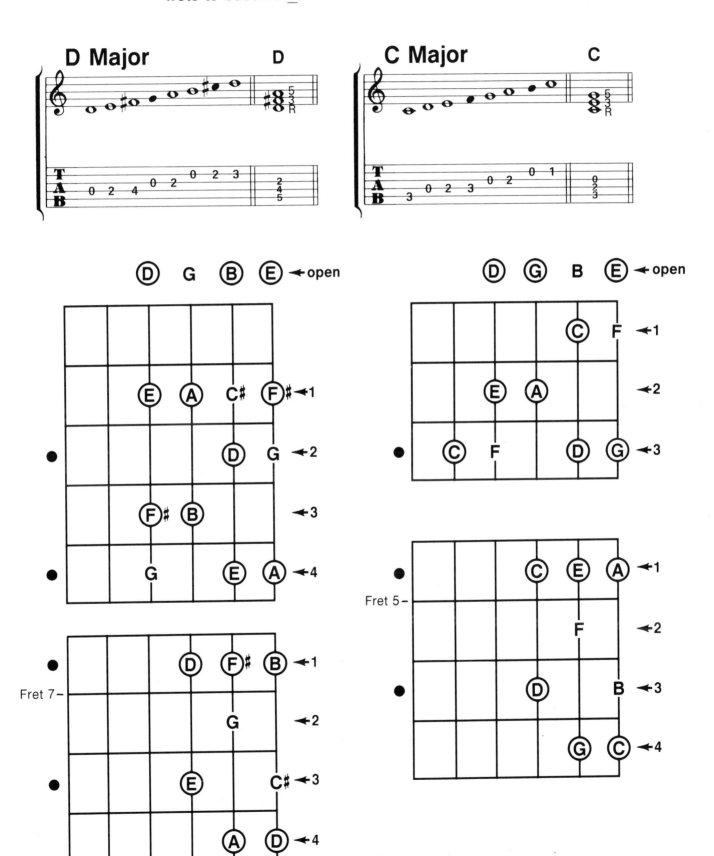

Rock Trax #7: Solo Licks

Think of the pentatonic notes (1 2 3 5 & 6) as the skeleton of the major scale. Use these notes as the skeleton of your improvisations, but add tones 4 and 7 for variety. Practice improvising at both positions on the neck.

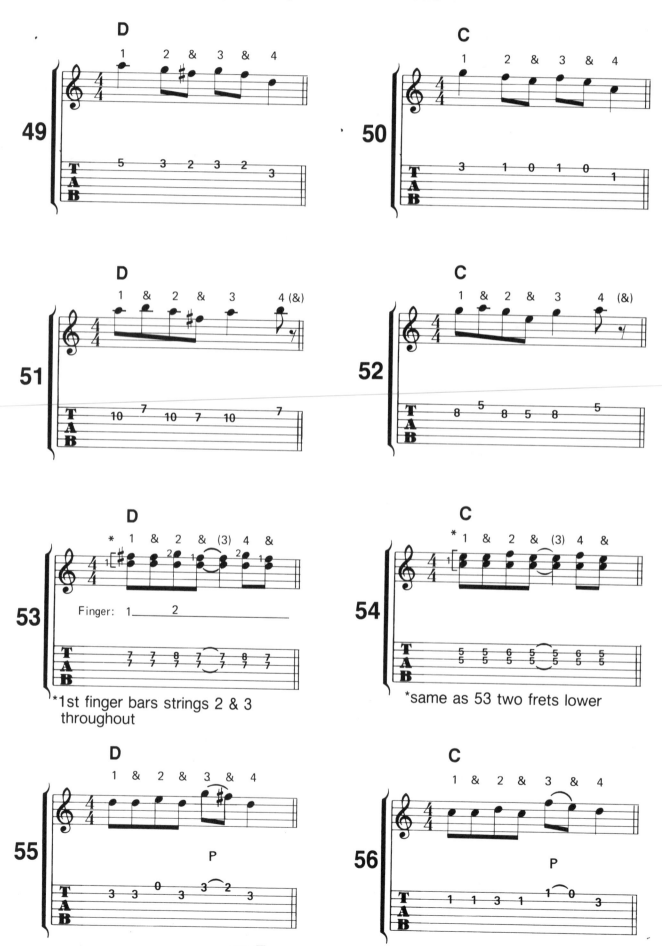

*1st finger bars strings 2 & 3 throughout

*same as 53 two frets lower

Rock Trax #8: Rhythm Guitar

The chords used in **Rock Trax #8** are chords you already know — **A, G,** and **D.** Play the Rock Strum below with the cassette/CD using various forms of the chords.

Rock Strum:

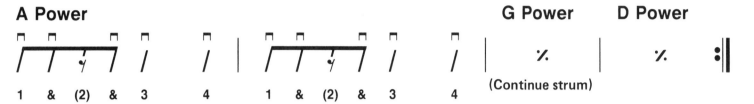

Rock Trax #8: Lead Guitar

You already studied lead scale patterns for the **G Chord** (page 168) and the **D Chord** (page 171), so the major scale, pentatonic and chord is given for the **A Chord** below. Study the patterns in both positions.

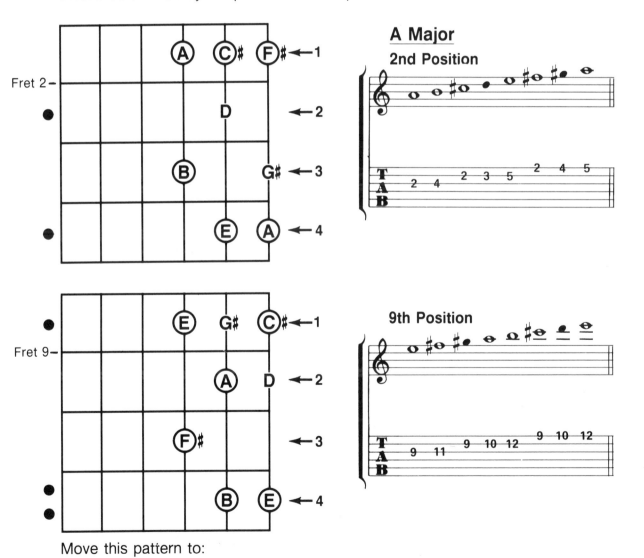

Move this pattern to:

Fret 7   **becomes G**
Fret 2   **becomes D**

Rock Trax #8: Solo Licks

Fretboard Tip: Many of the licks below can be moved to other positions of the fretboard for use with other chords.

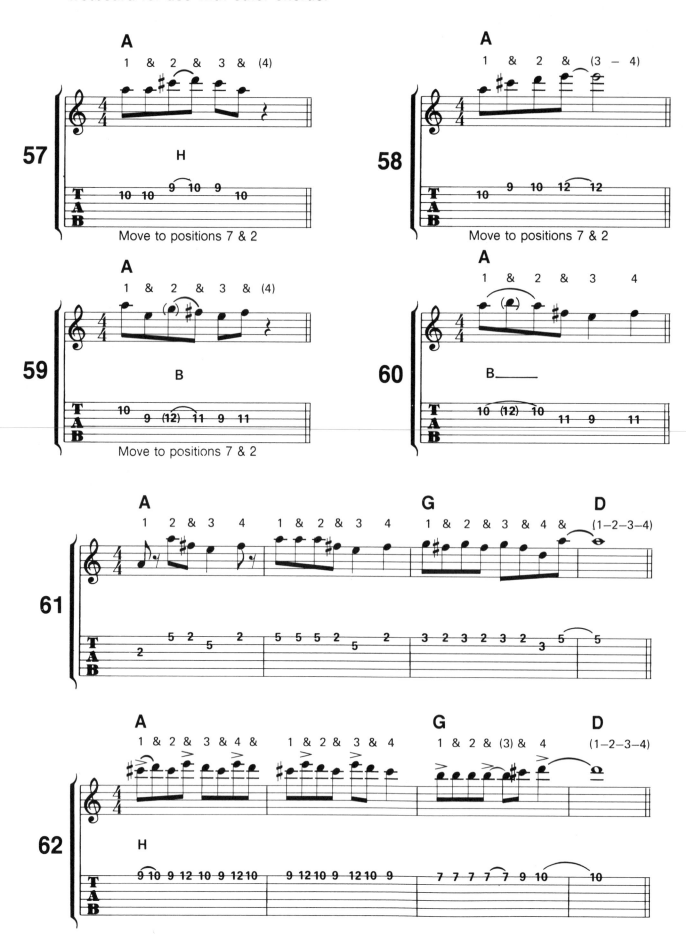

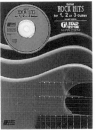

THE GUITAR TECHNIQUES SERIES

The series designed to get you started! Each book clearly presents essential concepts, highlighting specific elements of guitar playing and music theory. Most books include tablature and standard notation.

Acoustic Rock For Guitar

The acoustic guitar has found renewed popularity in contemporary rock. From ballads to metal, you'll find many artists adding that distinctive acoustic sound to their songs. This book demonstrates the elements of good acoustic guitar playing – both pick and fingerstyle – that are used in rock today. Topics include Chords and Variations, Strumming Styles, Picking Patterns, Scales and Runs, and much more.
00699327.....................................$6.95

Arpeggios For Guitar

An introduction to the basics, including: Performance etudes; one-octave arpeggios; five-and six-string forms; string-skipping forms; and more.
00695044 ....$6.95

Basic Blues For Guitar

This book taps into the history of great blues guitarists like B.B. King and Muddy Waters. It teaches the guitarist blues accompaniments, bar chords and how to improvise leads.
00699008 ....$6.95

Music Theory For Guitar

Music theory is the cornerstone in understanding music. But how does a guitar player relate it to the guitar? This volume answers that question. Concepts of scale, harmony, chords, intervals and modes are presented in the context of applying them to the guitar. This book will open the door to not only understanding the fundamentals of music, but also the world of playing the guitar with more insight and intelligence.
00699329.....................................$7.95

Finger Picks For Guitar

A convenient reference to 47 fingerstyle guitar accompaniment patterns for use with all types of music. In standard notation and tablature. Also includes playing tips.
00699125 ....$6.95

Lead Blues Licks

This book examines a number of blues licks in the styles of such greats as B.B. King, Albert King, Stevie Ray Vaughan, Eric Clapton, Chuck Berry, and more. Varying these licks and combining them with others can improve lead playing and can be used in rock styles as well as blues. Clearly written in notes and tab, you'll progress from the standard blues progression and blues scale to the various techniques of bending, fast pull offs and hammer-ons, double stops, and more.
00699325.....................................$6.95

Lead Rock Licks For Guitar

Learn the latest hot licks played by great guitarists, including Jeff Beck, Neal Schon (of Journey), Andy Summers (Police), and Randy Rhoads (Ozzy Osbourne). The guitarist can use each lick in this book as building material to further create new and more exciting licks of their own.
00699007 ....$6.95

Rhythms For Blues For Guitar

This book brings to life everything you need to play blues rhythm patterns, in a quick, handy and easy-to-use book. Everything from basic blues progressions to turnarounds, including swing, shuffle, straight eighths rhythms, plus small, altered and sliding chord patterns. All are presented in the style of many of the great blues and rock blues legends. Includes notes and tab.
00699326.....................................$6.95

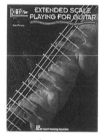

Extended Scale Playing For Guitar

An innovative approach to expanding left hand technique by Joe Puma. The sliding first finger technique presented in this book will give players a new and broader outlook on the guitar. The book explores a variety of scales – major, minor, half-tone/whole-tone – and more.
00697237.....................................$7.95

Right Hand Techniques

Through basic alternate, sweep and cross picking patterns, 10 chord arpeggios, palm muting and fingerstyle techniques, this book presents everything you need to know in getting started with the basic techniques needed to play every type of music. Additional topics include rhythm, rake and fingerstyle techniques. A real power packed technique book!
00699328.....................................$6.95

Rock Chords For Guitar

Learn to play open-string, heavy metal power chords and bar chords with this book. This book introduces most of the chords needed to play today's rock 'n' roll. There are very clear fingering diagrams and chord frames on the top of each page. Empty staves at the bottom of each page allow the player to draw in his own chord patterns.
00689649 ....$6.95

Rock Scales For Guitar

This book contains all of the Rock, Blues, and Country scales employed in today's music. It shows the guitarist how scales are constructed and designed, how scales connect and relate to one another, how and where to use the scales they are learning, all of the possible scale forms for each different scale type, how to move each scale to new tonal areas and much, much more.
00699164 ....$6.95

Strums For Guitar

A handy guide that features 48 guitar strumming patterns for use with all styles of music. Also includes playing tips.
00699135 ....$6.95

FOR MORE INFORMATION, SEE YOUR LOCAL MUSIC DEALER,
OR WRITE TO:

HAL•LEONARD® CORPORATION

7777 W. BLUEMOUND RD. P.O. BOX 13819 MILWAUKEE, WI 53213

Prices, book contents & availability subject to change without notice.

0796